THE INSPIRED WISDOM OF LALLA YOGESHWARI

THE INSPIRED WISDOM OF LALLA YOGESHWARI

A COMMENTARY ON THE MYSTICAL POETRY OF THE GREAT YOGINI OF KASHMIR

SWAMI NIRMALANANDA GIRI
(ABBOT GEORGE BURKE)

My Guru gave me but one percept:
"From without withdraw your gaze within
And fix it on the Inmost Self."
Taking to heart this one precept,
Naked I began to dance.
(Vakh 21)

LIGHT of the SPIRIT
PRESS
CEDAR CREST, NEW MEXICO

Published by
Light of the Spirit Press
lightofthespiritpress.com

Light of the Spirit Monastery
P. O. Box 1370
Cedar Crest, New Mexico 87008
OCOY.org

ISBN-13: 978-1-955046-15-2
Library of Congress Control Number: 2023932012
Light of the Spirit Press, Cedar Crest, New Mexico

First Edition 2023

BISAC Categories:
OCC010000   BODY, MIND & SPIRIT / Mindfulness & Meditation
REL032030   RELIGION / Hinduism / Sacred Writings
REL032010   RELIGION / Hinduism / History
03182023

CONTENTS

Dedicated to the happy and revered memory of
Sri Swami Rama of Hardwar (Ram Kunj)
To whom I bow again and again.

SOHAM

PREFACE

My Guru gave me but one precept:
"From without withdraw your gaze within
And fix it on the Inmost Self."
Taking to heart this one precept,
Naked I began to dance.

(Vakh 21)

Lalla Yogeshwari, also known as Lalleshwari or Lal Ded (Mother Lalla), was a great fourteenth-century yogini of Kashmir. She created a form of mystic poetry called Vatsun or Vakhs (from the Sanskrit *Vak*, which means Speech) that were the earliest compositions in the Kashmiri language. Lalla's poems are some of the earliest known works of Kashmiri literature. They were first written down in the twentieth century, until then having been memorized and spoken or sung only. The text of Lalla's Vakhs which I have used for this commentary is that by Jayalal Kaul which you can find posted at http://ikashmir.net/lalded/vakhs.html.

There is almost nothing known about her, though legends have abounded, most of them very like a hallucinogenic *Alice In Wonderland*. What is commonly believed is that she was born in 1326, a daughter of a Kashmiri Brahmin named Cheta Bhat, near Pampore, Kashmir, and was married at the age of twelve in accordance with the local customs. Following her marriage, she was renamed, as was the custom, Padmavati, but continued to be known as Lalla or Lal Ded. She seems to have left home sometime between the ages of twenty-four and twenty-six, to become a disciple of a spiritual leader, Siddha Srikanth (Sed Boyu), who was a Shaivite yogi. From then on she wandered, living on alms and became a teacher and spiritual leader herself. She was universally considered as a supreme siddha (perfected yogini) during her lifetime and afterward.

Lalla was in the tradition of the Nath Yogi Sampradaya whose meditation practice is that of Soham Sadhana: the joining of the mental repetition of Soham Mantra with the natural breath. (The mental intonation of the syllable *So* when inhaling and the mental intonation of the syllable *Ham* ["Hum"] when exhaling.) She will be referring to this practice in some of the Vakhs. (Soham Sadhana is the subject of my two books *Soham Yoga: The Yoga of the Self* and *Light of Soham*.)

I am mentioning this right at the beginning because an accurate understanding of Lallaji's words is not possible unless they are studied in the context of her personal sadhana–Soham Sadhana, the Original Yoga first taught publicly by the Nath Yogi Masters, Sri Matsyendranath and Yogi Guru Sri Gorakhnath.

Now Lalla herself can speak to us over the centuries.

Swami Nirmalananda Giri

The Vakhs of Lalla Yogeshwari

1.

With a rope of loose-spun thread am I towing my boat
upon the sea.
Would that God heard my prayer and brought me safe
across!
Like water in cups of unbaked clay I run to waste.
Would God I were to reach my home!

See how different are these words of a perfect paramhansa yogini
from the self-congratulatory boasts of false yogis and gurus
that love to spin poetic rhapsodies of their supreme realization
for the admiration of their hearers and readers! She honestly and
clearly describes the condition of all who find themselves in the
ocean of samsara we call "the world." And although established in
the non-dual state of nirvikalpa samadhi, she is keenly aware of
the difference between herself and Brahman the Absolute, and of
her utter dependence on Brahman as the essence of her existence
as a conscious entity.

*With a rope of loose-spun thread am I towing my boat upon the
sea.* The "rope of loose-spun thread" is the store of our accumulated

karmas, positive, negative and neutral. The boat of our life is being propelled upon the sea of continual birth and death by the force of those karmas. They are tenuous (loose-spun) because although karma is an absolute, it yet can be directed and modified by subsequent actions (karmas), especially by the practice of Soham yoga sadhana.

Everything that happens to us from life to life is not from outside ourselves, but from within, for karma is a creation of our will and our desires, our attachments, our attractions (raga) and our aversions (dwesha). Therefore we are towing our own boat of our embodiment in this world. Everything that happens to us is in a sense all done to us by ourselves through the karmic force we have set in motion in the past and which has created our present. Everything anyone has done to us in this life is exactly what we have done to others in a previous life. When Jesus said, "All things whatsoever ye would that men should do to you, do ye even so to them" (Matthew 7:12), he was not giving some noble ideal, some "golden rule" of high virtue, but was telling us how to create our karma: what we want to be done to us we should do to others.

The ego does not want to admit the truth that our own actions come back to us exactly in the actions and words of others toward us. People who cannot face their own negativity become very upset at hearing this truth spoken. Once someone wrote asking me why people were sexually molested in their childhood. I wrote back the truth: those who are sexually molested in their childhood have molested children themselves in a previous life. Explosion! I was summarily informed that she was molested in childhood so she would be able to help those who had been so molested. God save us from such saviors! I have known several people who believed in karma but adamantly refused to even consider that negative things came to them because it was their own past-life negativity returning to them. This is a trait of serious spiritual sociopathy.

On the positive side is the fact that great positive spiritual karma is created by us through Soham meditation, spiritual study, good deeds and a genuine positive attitude toward others. But especially through Soham meditation.

Would that God heard my prayer and brought me safe across! Here we see that Lalla is no simplistic book-advaitin who does not realize that although her Self is eternal and one with Brahman, it is finite and Brahman is infinite–and therefore she is utterly dependent on the Absolute. References to God hearing prayers and answering them is usually considered a characteristic of the followers of bhakti, and it is when it is meant in a childish, dualistic sense. But Lalla is a perfect jnani who sees the relationship of the finite with the Infinite in a correct perspective. They are one, but not the same (identical), they are different–distinct from one another–but not separate. Only the yogi really comprehends this, for it is a matter of perception-experience, not mere intellectual conceptualization. Nevertheless we see that Lalla prays to the Infinite and fully believes that she can be delivered from the ocean of samsara by the action of God–for this is the only way it can happen, since all occurs according to the divine order which is itself a manifestation of God. Lalla clearly sees the One in two, and the two in One. "This is the knowledge above all other: purifier and king of secrets, only made plain to the eye of the mystic" (Bhagavad Gita 9:2).

Like water in cups of unbaked clay I run to waste. Lalla means that without the insight she has just expressed, instead of remaining in unity with the Absolute she would become merged with samsara in ignorance, for water in unbaked clay eventually becomes absorbed by it and only a worthless mess remains. Wise are those who know the perils of immersion in relative consciousness to the exclusion of the true knowledge of the Self.

Would God I were to reach my home! Even an enlightened person cannot be fully at rest in the world because the Self is alien to this world. It belongs in the depths of the Absolute, not floating about in the fluctuations of samsara. The Self is essentially real and the world of relative existence is essentially unreal–illusory. So although the liberated person may rest in the Self, there is still a shadow of his dislocation from the transcendental realm. For all of us the situation is like that described in the poem in Mahler's Second ("Resurrection") Symphony.

> Man lies in greatest need!
> Man lies in greatest pain!
> How I would rather be in heaven.
> There came I upon a broad path
> When came a little angel
> And wanted to turn me away.
> Ah no! I would not let myself be turned away!
> I am from God and shall return to God!
> The loving God will grant me a little light,
> Which will light me into that eternal blissful life!

2.

I will weep and weep for you, O Mind;
The world has caught you in its spell.
Though you cling to them with the anchor of steel,
Not even the shadow of the things you love
will go with you when you are dead.
Why then have you forgotten your own true Self?

I will weep and weep for you, O Mind. On reading this sentence there came to my memory a high school classmate of mine that got his first teenage crush and spent a lot of time each day circling the block in his car in hopes of seeing his crushee through the windows of her house. At home he sat moping over his hopeless fixation for someone that literally did not know he existed. One of his aunts asked him what was the matter, and when he explained she commented, "Look, Jack, it is only in your head!" Where else would it be?

The mind is a wonderful thing, but also an overwhelming source of misery. The yogi, being introspective and more sensitive to the ways and depths of his mind than ordinary people, especially knows this to be true. The mind being a field of fluidic energies, it is its nature to fluctuate constantly in response to inner and outer conditions. And since we are not the mind but only its witness, however much we may identify with it, we are its observer and certainly may "weep and weep" for it and over it, both pitying it and pitying ourselves for our vulnerability to its instability and vagaries.

The world has caught you in its spell. Everything in relative existence consists of magnetic energies continually interacting with one another. The magnetic field of the mind immediately attaches itself to anything that vibrates in sympathy with it, and only with effort can it detach itself from something. It is like trying to pry apart two powerful magnets that have clamped on to one another. The interaction of the mind with the world outside itself is fundamentally a matter of polarities–attraction and repulsion. These two forces are called raga and dwesha by the yogis. The confusion that can be created by their alternating presence is virtually impossible to resolve.

The yogi must therefore become established in viveka and vairagya. Viveka is discrimination between the Real and the unreal, between the Self and the non-Self, between the permanent and the impermanent–right intuitive discrimination. Vairagya is non-attachment; detachment; dispassion; absence of desire; disinterest; or indifference–indifference towards and disgust for all worldly things and enjoyments.

This diagnosis and recommended cure is drastic, but what is more drastic than finding ourselves in this world without a clue as to how and why? Only those who can even conceive of breaking through this imprisonment may hope to find the way to freedom. Certainly there is cause for weeping when we consider the agony and tears of the lifetimes through which we have already suffered.

Though you cling to them with the anchor of steel, not even the shadow of the things you love will go with you when you are dead. A ship's anchor works by hooking itself on to an immovable object on the ocean floor. To be safe the chain and anchor must both be of steel that cannot rust or break. But Lalla tells us the truth: even if our attachment and desire to hold to them are made of the steel of the mind and will, not even their shadow will go with us through the gates of death. At the time of her death Queen Elizabeth I said, "All my possessions for a moment of time!" But the bargain was not struck.

Why then have you forgotten your own true Self? This is certainly a rhetorical question, because in the history of humanity no one has not forgotten the true Self. The necessary question is: *How will we remember our true Self?* And there is only one true answer: Soham yoga.

3.

There is a yawning pit underneath you, and you are
    dancing overhead.
Pray, Sir, how can you bring yourself to dance?
See, of the riches you are amassing here, nothing of
    them will go with you.
Pray, Sir, how can you relish your food and drink?

There is a yawning pit underneath you, and you are dancing overhead. The inescapable, yawning pit of death is beneath us awaiting our eventual descent into it. The moment we were born we began moving toward the brink of that abyss. At every moment of our lives the death process has been going on in our bodies, even if it was sometimes the prelude to the formation of new flesh or attributes. We have to die in this way to keep on living, but the final end of life is death itself. It wins out in the end

Pray, Sir, how can you bring yourself to dance? It takes a great deal of deliberate unawareness to keep on absorbed in the dance that takes us over the edge of life into death. "I want to live!" is a foolish and futile ambition when the purpose of life is unknown or ignored, and we continue in the ways that can only end in the pit.

See, of the riches you are amassing here, nothing of them will go with you. People pass their lives getting things, all of which must be left behind at death–if they have even been with them that long. We begin with nothing and end with nothing. And in getting these things we have violated our true nature as the Self and sown karmic seeds that will bring more bondage and more frustration in this life and future lives. A terrible investment!

Pray, Sir, how can you relish your food and drink? Years ago I read a description of how a pig considers himself the apex of existence. He has a nice sty in which to wallow, a wife and children, and someone who comes and feeds him every day. Surely he is the center of the universe, its chosen favorite. But all the time on the wall of the farmer whom he considers his faithful servant and benefactor there hangs a great, sharp knife with which that farmer will one day kill him. The pig has an excuse for such thinking, but what excuse do we have who see death around us from our childhood and yet give no thought to our inevitable fate?

4.

A wooden bow and rush grass for an arrow:
A carpenter unskilled and a palace to build:
A shop unlocked in a busy bazaar:
A body uncleansed by waters holy–
Oh dear! who knows what has befallen me?

Lalla now describes herself and everyone else in this world.

A wooden bow and rush grass for an arrow. In ancient India bows were made of horn (buffalo or rhinoceros were preferred) or steel, compared to which wood was not as flexible and therefore not as capable of shooting as far as the horn and steel bows. Furthermore the wooden bows were subject to moisture that could make them flaccid and dehydration that could make them brittle and easily broken. Rush grass was just that: grass (not reeds) from which it was impossible to fashion an arrow. A wooden bow and rush grass for an arrow–such is the human being which is fragile and unable to meet the harsh forces of the world effectually, much less conquer or master them. In other words such a person is helpless and hopeless in the "battle of life" so glibly spoken about. And he is defenseless against the forces of inner and outer illusion.

A carpenter unskilled and a palace to build. The destiny of the human being is divinity–the passage from a mud or thatch hut to a royal palace, symbolically speaking. But we do not know how to build such a structure. Here, too, we are helpless and hopeless. Worse than useless.

A shop unlocked in a busy bazaar. Such a place will be looted by whoever sees its unlocked condition. In the same way the heedless person who has not taken refuge in spiritual life and wisdom will have everything stolen from him by the forces of this troubled world. Although the treasure of divinity is within him, the samsarin is daily looted by the thieves of illusion and delusion, by the passions without number. He will be tormented and ultimately destroyed from life to life by the five enemies–lust (kama), anger (krodha), greed (lobha), delusion (moha), and envy (matsarya)–and drowned by the six waves of the ocean of samsara–hunger and thirst, old age and death, grief and delusion/loss of consciousness. What will be left of him to salvage? And it will continue from life to life to life.

A body uncleansed by waters holy. I never really have ascribed to the statement "only in a healthy body can you have a healthy mind," but there is truth in it, though not an absolute. And the same thing could be said about our environment, including our body. A daily life that has not been cleansed and purified by the continual presence of holiness in many forms is a life that is unavoidably unholy, however it may appear to us and others.

True Hindus (Sanatana Dharmis) worship God daily and drink the offered water (tirtha) afterward. Often they have water brought from the sacred Ganges which they drink and sprinkle to purify both themselves and their surroundings. And if possible they all wish to bathe at least once in the sacred Ganges, Yamuna, Kaveri, Narmada, and Godavari rivers as well as the Triveni, where the Ganges, Yamuna and Saraswati rivers come together. Having bathed in them all except for the Godavari I can testify to the benefits gained. Of course the Ganges is not just sacred, it is a divine manifestation. The first time I saw it I nearly fell in because

I knew that I was seeing divine consciousness in the form of water. And bathing in the Triveni was one of the most important events in my life.

Oh dear! who knows what has befallen me? It is called samsara. "Therefore be a yogi" (Bhagavad Gita 6:46).

5.

By the highway I came,
But by the highway I return not.
And so I find me still on the embarkment,
not having gone even half the way,
And the day is done, the light has failed.
I search my pockets but not a cowrie find:
What shall I pay for the ferry fee?

By the highway I came, but by the highway I return not. We come into this world from higher (astral) worlds by the way of birth, but we return by death.

And so I find me still on the embarkment, not having gone even half the way. Most people (non-yogis) find themselves still enmeshed in ordinary life, not having progressed even half way to birth in a higher world after leaving this one.

And the day is done, the light has failed. Youth with its vigor and optimism and confidence has gone, and the shadows of evening, the eventual night and the journey of death is coming of a surety.

I search my pockets but not a cowrie find. We take stock of our life and weigh up its entire span in hope of finding something gained that will ensure a painless and peaceful departure.

What shall I pay for the ferry fee? But after death when we are ourselves put in the balance of karma and destiny, what will we have within ourselves that will gain us an easy passage over and the possibility of never returning here?

6.

Ah me! the five, the ten,
And the eleventh, their lord the mind,
scraped this pot and went away.
Had all together pulled on the rope,
Why should the eleventh have lost the cow?

Ah me! the five, the ten, and the eleventh, their lord the mind,.... The five are the five bodies (koshas), corresponding to the five elements: ether (akasha), air (vayu), fire (agni), water (ap), and earth (prithvi), in which all sentient beings are encased. They are: Anandamaya kosha: the sheath of bliss (ananda), the causal body (karana sharira). Jnanamaya kosha: the sheath of intellect (buddhi), the level of intelligent thought and conceptualization, the astral-causal body. Manomaya kosha: the sheath of the mind (manas–mental substance), the level of the sensory mind, the astral body. Pranamaya kosha: the sheath of vital air (prana), consisting of vital forces and the (psychic) nervous system, including the senses. Annamaya kosha: the sheath of physical matter. The ten are the ten indriyas, the five organs of perception (jnanendriyas)–ear, skin, eye, tongue and nose–and the five organs of action (karmendriyas)–voice, hand, foot, organ of excretion and the organ of generation. The eleventh, the ruler/co-ordinator of these ten, is the intelligent, thinking mind itself: the intellect (buddhi).

Scraped this pot and went away. By "this pot" Lalla means her physical body which was ruled and conditioned by the eleven which in turn "went away" by the waning of their powers, especially through the ravages and degeneration of age. In India a wandering monk carries a water vessel, usually made of a gourd or coconut shell, called a kamandalu. But my friend Anand Maharaj carried an earthen kamandalu. Having not seen one before, I asked him why he did not have the usual kind. "Because this reminds me of the body made of earth that can be 'broken' at any time." He was certainly a disciple of Lalla.

Had all together pulled on the rope, why should the Eleventh have lost the cow? The rope is the "rope of loose-spun thread," mentioned in the first verse, by which Lalla was towing her boat upon the sea of samsara, endeavoring to pass through this world by means of yogic enlightenment which is here referred to as "the cow." In the scriptural language of Hinduism, Sanskrit, the syllable *go* means both a ray of light and a cow. Lalla uses "cow" in this symbolic sense. If the eleven had all together pulled on the rope at the will of Lalla, then the mind would not have lost its illumination. But it did, and Lalla put forth her will at full intensity to catch hold of and retain the light. Although she had done so successfully, she laments having needed to go to such trouble and struggle. This is the perspective of any serious yogi. It value lies in the setting of yogi's will to make sure that "the cow" never gets away again.

7.

Forever we come, forever we go;
Forever, day and night, we are on the move.
Whence we come, thither we go,
Forever in the round of birth and death,
From nothingness to nothingness.
But sure, a mystery here abides,
A Something is there for us to know.

Forever we come, forever we go. This verse is about those who are immersed in samsara and its delusions which we call maya. Impermanence and constant change are its attributes, and so are the lives and minds of those in its influence. In Hebrew the word for samsara means "rolling" in the sense of constant movement and instability. So is all relative existence.

Human beings are in the grip of the dualities, the dwandwas, the pairs of opposites inherent in nature (prakriti) such as pleasure and pain, hot and cold, light and darkness, gain and loss, victory and defeat, attraction and aversion, happiness and sorrow, birth and death. They are the waves of the ocean of samsara which perpetually rise and fall, move back and forth, sometimes calm and sometimes stormy.

Forever, day and night, we are on the move. Since the external aspect of us is part of prakriti, we never stop being "on the move."

Whence we come, thither we go, forever in the round of birth and death. We come from disembodiment into embodiment and back into disembodiment over and over again caught in that duality. "Thus they are seen, and appear unceasingly,... returning back to the new birth, new death: all helpless" (Bhagavad Gita 8:19). "Helpless all, for Maya is their master" (Bhagavad Gita 9:8).

From nothingness to nothingness. This has two meanings. Since nothing lasts, it is ultimately "nothing" essentially, and since maya is appearance only, even the appearance of birth and death are nothing. It reminds me of Thales the ancient Greek philosopher who taught that life and death are the same. When asked why he did not commit suicide and die he replied: "Because it would make no difference."

In a sense karma is also nothing because at first it does not exist, then it is created, then it is fulfilled and ceases to exist for us. So we go from nothingness to nothingness as Lalla says. Further the Gita admonishes us: "Do not say: 'God gave us this delusion.' You dream you are the doer, you dream that action is done, you dream that action bears fruit. It is your ignorance, it is the world's delusion that gives you these dreams" (Bhagavad Gita 5:14). Of course a dream does take place and at that time is real, but when we awake it is no more than an idea in our mind—so it exists but is not real! Therefore our idea of the nature of existence itself is an error, since we attribute it to that which never exists in our ignorance of the reality that is our Self which does exist. (You might want to read that over!)

Perhaps we should think of our situation as sitting in a motion picture theater. If we look at the pictures on the screen we are looking at something that is basically nothing and non-existent. But we can look around and see the others watching with us that are real and do exist. The movie will end and disappear, but the viewers will not.

The Gita should have the last word on this: "That which is non-existent can never come into being, and that which is can never cease to be. Those who have known the inmost Reality know also the nature of *is* and *is not*" (Bhagavad Gita 2:16).

But sure, a mystery here abides, a Something is there for us to know. And if we do not know it our life counts for nothing. We must know by our yogic experience the truth of the following verses of the Gita.

"Bodies are said to die, but That which possesses the body is eternal" (Bhagavad Gita 2:18).

"Know this Atman unborn, undying, never ceasing, never beginning, deathless, birthless" (Bhagavad Gita 2:20)

"Not wounded by weapons, not burned by fire, not dried by the wind, not wetted by water: such is the Atman, not dried, not wetted, not burned, not wounded, innermost element, everywhere, always, being of beings, changeless, eternal, for ever and ever" (Bhagavad Gita 2:23-24).

We must know the Self.

8.

Whence I have come and by which way, I do not know.
Whither I shall go and by which way, I do not know.
Were I to know the end of it all and gain the knowledge
of the truth,
It would be well, for otherwise life here is but an empty
breath.

So there is something we must do: Soham yoga sadhana in which we fill the breath with Soham: intoning *So* when we inhale and *Ham* ("Hum") when we exhale naturally. Again and again.

9.

I have seen a learned man die of hunger,
A sere leaf drop in winter wind;
I have seen an utter fool beat his cook
[Who could not make a toothsome dish].
Since then I, Lalla, anxiously await
The day when the lure of the world will fall away.

I have seen a learned man die of hunger, a sere [dry] leaf drop in winter wind. The man's learning could not prevent his death from poverty, but became as nothing more than a dead, dry leaf blown by the wind. Many times renowned or oppressive people have died, and those who saw them marveled that they looked so insubstantial or inconsequential, although many had respected or feared them when they were alive.

I have seen an utter fool beat his cook [who could not make a toothsome dish.] Lalla saw how worthless people could become oppressors of those who did not fulfil their will, and how those oppressed could do nothing about the situation but endure it, even though the mistreatment was capricious and far more severe than the failure merited. So it has always been between the powerful and the weak, the "high" and the "low." Inequality and injustice are common, especially for those considered of no consequence in a society.

Since then I, Lalla, anxiously await the day when the lure of the world will fall away. Swami Vivekananda said that the world is like a dog's curly tail—it cannot be straightened by any means. Lalla saw that the attraction of the world for the mind was the same way, and yearned for the time when the world would be as nothing to her.

10.

Now I saw a stream flowing;
Now neither bank nor bridge was seen.
Now I saw a bush in bloom;
Now neither rose nor thorn was seen.

11.

Now I saw the hearth ablaze,
Now I saw not fire nor smoke.
Now I saw the Pandava Mother,
Now she was but a potters' aunt.

Here again Lalla is faced with nothingness as the nature of this world. The world is like a magician: now you see it—now you don't. At first you think there is something meaningful, lasting or substantial in a situation, an attainment or a person. Then suddenly you see the nothingness and realize it was nothing from the first, only you did not see beyond the momentary appearance of it or the mistaken conclusions you drew about it.

12.

A royal fly-whisk, sunshade, chariot and throne,

Merry revels, pleasures of the theater, a bed of cotton
down–

Which of these, you think, will go with you when you
are dead?

How then can you dispel the fear of death?

A royal fly-whisk, sunshade [umbrella], chariot and throne...
These things are signs of royalty and therefore privilege and power,
insubstantial and superficial though they be. Yet these things were
jealously guarded in India. Early in the twentieth century there
were riots in south India because some low caste people bought and
used cotton umbrellas made in England, thus supposedly usurping
the privilege and rank of their "betters" and violating the long-es-
tablished social order. Was anybody reading the Bhagavad Gita?

Merry revels, pleasures of the theater, a bed of cotton down....
These things are only of the moment, their very nature is to end in
a short while, and therefore have virtually no significance or value.

Which of these, you think, will go with you when you are dead?
They truly are here today and gone tomorrow–as are the bodies
we call "me."

How then can you dispel the fear of death? Through possessions
and privilege we live as we please, blind to the fact that they can be
taken from us at any moment, especially by our inevitable death.

As the wise Solomon said: "Vanity of vanities, saith the
Preacher, vanity of vanities; all is vanity [*hebel*: that which leads
one astray; emptiness].... I have seen all the works that are done

under the sun; and, behold, all is vanity and vexation of spirit.... Therefore I hated life; because the work that is wrought under the sun is grievous unto me: for all is vanity and vexation of spirit.... For that which befalleth the sons of men befalleth beasts; even one thing befalleth them: as the one dieth, so dieth the other; yea, they have all one breath; so that a man hath no preeminence above a beast: for all is vanity" (Ecclesiastes 1:2, 14; 2:17, 19).

Yet there is a positive side, once we see the vanity of all that eventually passes way. So Theodore Tilton wrote in his poem *Even This Shall Pass Away*:

> Once In Persia reigned a king,
> Who upon his signet ring
> Graved a maxim true and wise,
> Which, if held before his eyes,
> Gave him counsel at a glance
> Fit for every change and chance.
> Solemn words, and these are they;
> "Even this shall pass away."

> Trains of camels through the sand
> Brought him gems from Samarcand;
> Fleets of galleys through the seas
> Brought him pearls to match with these;
> But he counted not his gain
> Treasures of the mine or main;
> "What is wealth?" the king would say;
> "Even this shall pass away."

'Mid the revels of his court,
At the zenith of his sport,
When the palms of all his guests
Burned with clapping at his jests,
He, amid his figs and wine,
Cried, "O loving friends of mine;
Pleasures come, but not to stay;
Even this shall pass away."

Lady, fairest ever seen,
Was the bride he crowned his queen.
Pillowed on his marriage bed,
Softly to his soul he said:
"Though no bridegroom ever pressed
Fairer bosom to his breast,
Mortal flesh must come to clay–
Even this shall pass away."

Fighting on a furious field,
Once a javelin pierced his shield;
Soldiers, with a loud lament,
Bore him bleeding to his tent.
Groaning from his tortured side,
"Pain is hard to bear," he cried;
"But with patience, day by day,
Even this shall pass away."

Towering in the public square,
Twenty cubits in the air,
Rose his statue, carved in stone.
Then the king, disguised, unknown,
Stood before his sculptured name,
Musing meekly: "What is fame?
Fame is but a slow decay;
Even this shall pass away."

Struck with palsy, sore and old,
Waiting at the Gates of Gold,
Said he with his dying breath,
"Life is done, but what is Death?"
Then, in answer to the king,
Fell a sunbeam on his ring,
Showing by a heavenly ray,
"Even this shall pass away."

13.

Why have you sunk deep in the sea of the illusory plea-
    sures of the world?
Why have you pulled down the high-banked road which
    could have led you safe across?
The dense darkness of tamas surrounds you now, and, at
    the appointed time,
Yama's messengers prepare to drag your body bleeding
    to death.
Who can dispel your fear of death?

Why have you sunk deep in the sea of the illusory pleasures of the world? That is not a very hard question to answer. We are sunk deep in the sea of the illusory pleasures of the world because when we were born both the traumas of the womb-experience and the birth process–during both of which we experienced our mother's thoughts as our own including her fear and great pain at our birth–plunged us into material awareness to the exclusion any objective self-awareness. So to a great degree our conscious memory was blanked out and only our samskaras remained with us. But we also had to learn that we were not our mother, but a separate being about which we truly knew nothing. So we had to remember a lot from our previous life and work from there while learning from our present situation. Plus simple sensory experience completely filled our awareness and displaced any previous understanding of this world and the purpose of our being in it. Without our volition years of moment-by-moment experiences began flooding on (and into) us at every moment of every day. What else could we do but sink? Just "knowing better" was no deterrent while under the hypnotic control of externalized consciousness and experience. Unless we were in touch with our latent samskaras how could it be otherwise?

Why have you pulled down the high-banked road which could have led you safe across? Easy. We did not know it–or we did not recognize it for what it was. We did not willfully forget it, but in our many lives when we did encounter it, it did not make any sense to us. We had to make a lot of mistakes to get the idea there might be a better way than just running around like a heedless animal.

This reminds me of an experience I had when I was three or four years old. The grocery store in my little home town delivered groceries, and one day my grandmother was putting up the things she had ordered when she said to my mother, "Why this is vegetarian vegetable soup, but I ordered vegetable beef soup!" I heard this and asked, "What does 'vegetarian' mean?" My grandmother told me, "Vegetarians live in California and never eat meat." I thought they must be very silly people indeed! And now I am one. But it took a lot of learning before I learned that vegetarianism is an essential of the high-banked road, since diet and consciousness are inseparable and the energies of the mind are formed of the subtle energies of the food we eat. My family considered themselves Christians, followers of Jesus, but in the oldest text of the Gospels, which is in Aramaic, the language of Jesus, Jesus himself says, "Take care that you never make your hearts heavy by eating meat."

The dense darkness of tamas surrounds you now, and, at the appointed time, Yama's messengers prepare to drag your body bleeding to death. Yama is the Lord of Death, controller of who dies and what happens to them after death. He has many messengers who come for the departing soul and take them over into the astral world. Lalla's vivid words about bleeding do not usually apply, and the body she mentions is the astral body of the departed.

Who can dispel your fear of death? You yourself can do so by gaining the knowledge that there is no death through diligent Soham yoga sadhana in which your real nature becomes apparent. Further, through daily Soham meditation the bonds of the body and mind become lessened and death is as easy as changing your clothes, for "just as the dweller in this body passes through childhood, youth and old age, so at death he merely passes into another kind of body. The wise are not deceived by that.… Bodies are said to die, but That which possesses the body is eternal. It cannot be limited, or destroyed.… Worn-out garments are shed by the body: worn-out bodies are shed by the dweller within the body. New bodies are donned by the dweller, like garments" (Bhagavad Gita 2:13, 18, 22).

My mother and grandmother had something to do with my perceptions of death, also. I heard my grandmother and mother talking about going to the funeral. My question, "What's a funeral?" elicited the vague answer that it was a church service that was done when you died. "What's 'die'?" (They should have known that was coming.) Apparently they held the mistaken idea that it is morbid to tell little children about death, although one of the reasons the Lord Jesus told His disciples to become like little children (Mark 10:15) is their capacity for accepting realities–even if they do not completely comprehend them. Therefore I got no answer worth considering. Standing there in the kitchen I made an interesting decision: I would "see" for myself what death was. And since I did not "know" I could not–I did.

I saw a bed and an old lady lying on it. She seemed to be suffering from some cause. As I watched, she appeared to fall asleep, but simultaneously a translucent duplicate of the woman rose up out of her body. I understood that the duplicate was really "her," that she had gone out of her body just like I got out of my pajamas every morning. The "real" form began to rise upward right through the ceiling and roof of her house. She did not stop, but continued rising high, high above the town. When she got up into the clouds a golden light appeared and she went into it and was gone. I realized that she had gone "somewhere else" to continue living. I also realized that some version of this happened to everyone at the end of life, and that it would also happen to me. But I would still be alive, only in a different place.

One of the best expositions of immortality is the poem written by Emily Bronte only a few weeks before she died from tuberculosis.

No Coward Soul Is Mine

No coward soul is mine,
No trembler in the world's storm-troubled sphere:
I see Heaven's glories shine,
And Faith shines equal, arming me from Fear.

O God within my breast,
Almighty, ever-present Deity!
Life, that in me has rest,
As I, undying Life, have power in Thee!

Vain are the thousand creeds
That move men's hearts: unutterably vain;
Worthless as withered weeds,
Or idlest froth amid the boundless main,

To waken doubt in one
Holding so fast by Thy infinity,

So surely anchored on
The steadfast rock of Immortality.

With wide-embracing love
Thy Spirit animates eternal years,
Pervades and broods above,
Changes, sustains, dissolves, creates, and rears.

Though earth and moon were gone,
And suns and universes ceased to be,
And Thou wert left alone,
Every existence would exist in Thee.

There is not room for Death,
Nor atom that his might could render void:
Thou–thou art Being and Breath,
And what thou art may never be destroyed.

14.

Why do you dote upon someone, my Soul, who is not
   your true love?
Why have you taken the false for the true?
Why can't you understand, why can't you know?
It is ignorance that binds you to the false,
To the ever-recurring wheel of birth and death, this
   coming and going.

Why do you dote upon someone, my Soul, who is not your true love? Why have you taken the false for the true? Why can't you understand, why can't you know? Why are we attached to that which is ultimately nothing to us—and we are nothing to it? This includes objects, possessions, persons and nearly all the things that we consider part of our life. We truly are "dwellers in the mirage." But how is this possible, and how has it happened to us?

It is ignorance that binds you to the false, to the ever-recurring wheel of birth and death, this coming and going. Again: it is all a mirage. What we see and experience is real, but our interpretation and understanding of it is false. It is real, but we see and live it as a lie. And since this is all in our mind, the only remedy is also internal: the insight given to us through Soham meditation.

15.

O man, why do you twist a rope of sand?
You cannot tow your boat with it.
What God has written in karma's script
Cannot be altered or reversed.

O man, why do you twist a rope of sand? You cannot tow your boat with it. We became acquainted with this rope of sand in the first of Lalla's verses. It is the store of our accumulated karmas, positive, negative and neutral. Lalla, by the force of her yogic attainment, was able to tow her boat with it, but we who are samsarins cannot—though we should be wise and dedicate ourselves to Soham yoga sadhana as did Lalla. But at this time we cannot use knowledge of our karmas to direct our path in life, for we have no such knowledge. Therefore Lalla is speaking the truth to us when she says:

What God has written in karma's script cannot be altered or reversed. That is, the law of karma which is imbedded in the very fabric of the universe and our bodies, gross and subtle, can never be changed or "broken" by anyone. Even God does not abrogate the karmic laws. So we have to learn the means of our evolution by learning and following the divinely-written law and the universal principles behind them which we can employ intelligently in our life–which we can then transform through the alchemy of yoga and wisdom (jnana). Thus we create for ourselves the karma of enlightenment and reap the harvest of Self-realization.

16.

What was it you had sown which should have borne a
    rich harvest?
You had but tanned a carcass hide, shaped and stretched
    it taut on pegs,
(Your only care your own body which you pegged to the
    bonds of desire).
But counsel to a fool is labour lost,
Like a ball thrown at a big-sized pillar, rebounding but
    not hitting the mark;
Or fruitless as feeding a tawny bullock on sweet molas-
    ses,
And expect a yield of milk from him.

What was it you had sown which should have borne a rich harvest? Life is wasted by doing the wrong things in the wrong ways in the wrong places. So Lalla is asking us—knowing that we have not just sat in a corner and done nothing—what it was that we have occupied ourselves with all of our life up till now with no worthwhile results at all—just the opposite. We are paupers in the spirit, having "spent" our lives in vain pursuits. So she asks if we now realize what seeds we should have sown in our inner and outer life. For there is hope for us still if we turn ourselves into the right path and expend our time and energy in the ways of the Self.

You had but tanned a carcass hide, shaped and stretched it taut on pegs. Up till now we have really cared only about our bodies, looking after the external, even disciplining and altering it to conform to our wrong ideas about its and our reason for even being in the world.

But counsel to a fool is labour lost, like a ball thrown at a big-sized pillar, rebounding but not hitting the mark. Lalla speaks the truth to those she encounters, but they are old and skilled in foolishness if not in outright evil. So for her or us to advise or admonish them is a complete loss of time and effort which will rebound to us in the form of being ignored or our words misinterpreted and distorted and turned on us in justification for their folly, and their outright hatred and anger in indignant rejection of our words and efforts which they denounce as being foolish or evil, rather than they and their deeds and words being foolish or evil.

Or fruitless as feeding a tawny bullock on sweet molasses, and expect a yield of milk from him. Giving molasses to a heifer is considered a good way to increase the amount of milk they will produce. But to give it to a bullock is not just a total waste of time, it is insanity.

17.

In your mother's womb you vowed not to be born again.
When will you recall the vow and die, even while alive?
Great honor will be yours in this life and greater honor
after death.

In your mother's womb you vowed not to be born again. The Garbha Upanishad describes the various phases of the child's development in the womb. In the seventh month after conception, the soul receives knowledge of its past and future. It knows who it has been and who it will be, what it has suffered and what it will suffer. This profoundly disturbs and even frightens the child, so it begins calling on God for help, even begging or vowing not to be born in an earthly body again.

When will you recall the vow and die, even while alive? The subconscious memory of the vow taken in the womb exists in us in the form of a samskara in our subconscious. When will at least the subliminal memory of that vow manifest as an inner urge within us to avoid further birth and death and their attendant miseries? Now in the body, will we follow our resolve and keep our vow to ourself and God?

Great merit will be yours in this life and greater merit after death. If we do keep that urgent vow, we will have great merit in this life and even greater merit when we leave the body and rise to higher worlds beyond the possibility of falling back into this material world. Surely this is the fulfillment of of all righteousness.

18.

Impart not esoteric truth to fools,
Nor on molasses feed an ass.
Do not sow seed in sandy beds,
Nor waste your oil on cakes of bran.

Impart not esoteric truth to fools. This is a most important injunction for many reasons. 1) They will drive you crazy asking you over and over to explain, and looking at you blankly so you foolishly think you have failed to communicate with them so they still do not understand. 2) They will think you are yourself crazy or irrational or a fool and will say or act so and mock you and the wisdom you have spoken to them. 3) They will be outraged at you "confusing" them since they cannot understand what you said. And denunciation will not be far behind. 4) They will especially hate the esoteric truth that is the basis for disciplines, especially in diet and abstinence from harmful things such as alcohol, nicotine and mind-affecting substances. 5) They will pretend to accept what you say, but twist and pervert the truth you told them. For example, one fool claimed that the teaching of the Bhagavad Gita (2:19), "Some say this Atman is slain, and others call It the slayer: they know nothing. How can It slay or who shall slay It?" meant that abortion was not an act of murder. One man said to me several times, "I remember you once told me...," and then proceeded to say idiotic and outrageous things which I never thought or said in my life. The purpose of these fools? To take vengeance on you for telling them the truth. Remember: they may be fools, but that does not mean they are not also cunningly intelligent. And evil.

Nor on molasses feed an ass. As we have seen, molasses is fed to bullocks so they will grow to be strong and able to plow fields and carry very heavy loads. A donkey can do none of these things, so to feed them molasses is to waste it. And so it is with people who cannot use (apply) the wisdom you give them.

Do not sow seed in sandy beds. The seeds will germinate, but the plants that grow will be sickly, weak and soon die. The same will happen with the truth told to shallow and rootless people.

Nor waste your oil on cakes of bran. They are unfit for anything, as are the fools you should avoid.

Yogananda used to say, "Company is greater than will power." If you associate with fools you will eventually become one. Stay away.

19.

I might disperse the southern clouds,
I might drain out the sea,
I might cure the incurable sick,
But I cannot convince a fool.

This is simple truth that should be taken to heart. Do not waste your time with fools. I once went with a fool to meet a real yogi living in obscurity in California. At one point the yogi looked at me, smiling, and said, "Why carry around empty space?" I understood and followed his hint.

20.

What is bitter at first is sweet in the end,
What is sweet at first is poison in the end.
It all depends on the effort put in, and the unflagging
determined will;
For whoever strives must soon arrive at the city of his
choice.

What is bitter at first is sweet in the end. What is sweet at first is poison in the end. "Who knows the Atman knows that happiness born of pure knowledge: the joy of sattwa. Deep his delight after strict self-schooling: sour toil at first but at last what sweetness, the end of sorrow. Senses also have joy in their marriage with things of the senses, sweet at first but at last how bitter: steeped in rajas, that pleasure is poison" (Bhagavad Gita 18:37-38). In his vision recorded in the book of Revelation, Saint John saw an angel with a little book in his hand, representing true wisdom… "And I went unto the angel, and said unto him, Give me the little book. And he said unto me, Take it, and eat it up; and it shall make thy belly bitter, but it shall be in thy mouth sweet as honey. And I took the little book out of the angel's hand, and ate it up; and it was in my mouth sweet as honey: and as soon as I had eaten it, my belly was bitter" (Revelation 10:9-10). Sri Ramakrishna remarked that rock sugar is good for the liver, but it tastes bitter to a person with liver trouble. When I first consulted with Dr. Josef Lenninger, the great naturopath, he gave me a cup of clear liquid to drink. I did so and remarked that it tasted very good. "But if you had told me it tasted bad or bitter," he told me, "I would have known you have liver trouble." So "bitter medicine" is often needed by us in the search for truth.

It all depends on the effort put in, and the unflagging determined will. For whoever strives must soon arrive at the city of his choice. This is very true. The yogi's success or failure depends on the quality and quantity of his sadhana supported by an "unflagging and determined will." For whoever puts forth effort in valid spiritual pursuit shall attain his end in time and experience the liberation he has chosen as his place of permanent abode. "Seek refuge in the knowledge of Brahman" (Bhagavad Gita 2:49). "Strive without ceasing to know the Atman, seek this knowledge and comprehend clearly why you should seek it: such, it is said, are the roots of true wisdom" (Bhagavad Gita 13:11).

21.

My Guru gave me but one precept:
"From without withdraw your gaze within
And fix it on the Inmost Self."
Taking to heart this one precept,
Naked I began to dance.

In the Nath Yogi tradition God is the guru who is embodied in the Soham mantra. Lalla is relating to us what this Soham Guru directed her to do. The Gita says it very well: "Patiently, little by little, a man must free himself from all mental distractions, with the aid of the intelligent will. He must fix his mind upon the Atman, and never think of anything else" (Bhagavad Gita 6:25). He who follows this precept leaves all things behind and seeks the Self alone. "Naked" in his purpose and in the divesting of all other purpose or desire in his heart, he finds what he seeks and dances in his joyful freedom. "His mind is dead to the touch of the external: it is alive to the bliss of the Atman. Because his heart knows Brahman his happiness is for ever" (Bhagavad Gita 5:21). "When, through the practice of yoga, the mind ceases its restless movements, and becomes still, he realizes the Atman. It satisfies him entirely. Then he knows that infinite happiness which can be realized by the purified heart but is beyond the grasp of the senses. He stands firm in this realization. Because of it, he can never again wander from the inmost truth of his being" (Bhagavad Gita 6:20-21). "The abstinent run away from what they desire but carry their desires with them: when a man enters Reality, he leaves his desires behind him" (Bhagavad Gita 2:59). Blessed nudity!

22.

He who wields the sword a kingdom gains;
Heaven [Swarga] is gained by tapasya and alms.
Follow the Guru's word and gain
True knowledge of the Self within.
Of his own virtue and his sin
Man himself surely reaps the fruits.

He who wields the sword a kingdom gains. Many things can be a "sword," such as wisdom, will power and discrimination between the true and the false. That is why the Gita says: "Still I can see it: a doubt that lingers deep in your heart brought forth by delusion. You doubt the truth of the living Atman. Where is your sword, Discrimination? Draw it and slash delusion to pieces" (Bhagavad Gita 4:42). The most powerful sword is the ceaseless pursuit of Self-realization through yoga sadhana backed by our total will power and wisdom in wielding it. Those who persevere in using that sword will gain the kingdom of self-mastery and Self-realization.

Heaven [Swarga] is gained by tapasya and alms. A Brief Sanskrit Glossary defines tapasya: "Austerity; practical (i.e., result-producing) spiritual discipline; spiritual force. Literally it means the generation of heat or energy, but is always used in a symbolic manner, referring to spiritual practice and its effect, especially the roasting of karmic seeds, the burning up of karma." That highest good which is beyond this earthly realm is gained by intense Soham sadhana and self-purification through discipline, especially a strict vegetarian diet along with abstinence from nicotine, alcohol and mind-affecting substances.

Follow the Guru's word and gain true knowledge of the Self within. By practicing Soham sadhana according to the words of enlightened yogis, supported by the requisite purification and discipline, Self-realization is attained within the depths of the yogi's own consciousness-being.

Of his own virtue and his sin man himself surely reaps the fruits. We ourselves have created our karma through our own past right and wrong deeds, thoughts, desires and will. All that is "done" to us in this world is really our own doing returning to us. It is an echo–our own "voice"–and will reveal exactly the nature of our previous actions. There are no helpless victims, only reapers of what they themselves have sown in the past. The ego hates this truth, but it is truth, nonetheless. Those who cannot face up to their own responsibility and culpability have no possibility of spiritual attainment of any kind.

23.

The sling of my candy load has gone loose, (and it galls
    my back);
My body has bent double under its weight; how shall I
    carry the load?
The word of my Guru (that I must lose the world to gain
    my soul),
Has been a painful "loss-blister" for me.
I am become a shepherdless flock, ah me!

The sling of my candy load has gone loose, (and it galls my back). My body has bent double under its weight; how shall I carry the load? The folly of every human being is the outward search for pleasure, enjoyment and satisfaction, whereas fulfillment and happiness are found only within, in the Self. We keep accumulating the "sweet" things of life that are only pain and bitterness in the end. "Senses have joy in their marriage with things of the senses, sweet at first but at last how bitter: that pleasure is poison" (Bhagavad Gita 18:38).

We cannot continue to hold on to them, for although they are heavy and wear us raw in their getting and keeping, they must slip away from us, for they have nothing to do with the Self. And no matter how much we try to lie to ourselves and act as though the Self is not our only reality, we constantly experience misery and sorrow because the "things of the world" are not only alien to the Self, they destroy the possibility of our gaining awareness and knowledge of the Self. They are, indeed, our "beloved enemy" by our own choice and deed. We have pain and are bent under the deadly weight of our search for that which cannot be found anywhere but within. Our condition is intolerable for us, yet we cannot (will not) let go of it and be free.

The word of my Guru (that I must lose the world to gain my soul), has been a painful "loss-blister" for me. The truth of the liberated siddhas that we must let go of the world and our attachments to it is also a terrible pain to us. Miserable because of the world and miserable because we cannot stand the idea of letting go and turning from it: that is the sum of our "life" in the world.

I am become a shepherdless flock, ah me! We have lost control of ourselves and at the same time are driving ourselves in the desperate search for–and grasping after–the world, which can never be ours because it is outside us. We think we are in it, but that is only an illusory dream. We are seeking for that which cannot be found because it does not exist in light of the ultimate Reality. It is false, but we are real: this is the antithesis that torments us. But we will not give it up, nor will we "shepherd" ourselves through self-control, the disciplines of yama and niyama and tapasya–intense Soham sadhana.

24.

A thousand times my Guru I asked:
"How shall the Nameless be defined?"
I asked and asked but all in vain.
The Nameless Unknown, it seems to me,
Is the source of the something that we see.

A thousand times my Guru I asked: 'How shall the Nameless be defined?' I asked and asked but all in vain. Why? Because it was the wrong question. Buddha said that the right questions must first be asked before we can get the right answers. We ask a question because we do not know something, but we have to have some knowledge to even think of the right question. The sadhaka must possess a combination of intuition and intellect to make his search for truth possible.

A sadhaka must have all the qualifications before he can search for truth in a viable way that will ensure his finding the truth. We have to have a subtle inner knowing for us to reach the knowledge we seek. For example, we can ask someone we think is qualified to answer our questions, but at the same time we have to have the ability to discern whether the answers we get are true or sufficient. It takes insight to ask a question and understanding to determine if the answer is valid or complete. So we have to somehow know the answer before we do any asking. Samskara has a lot to do with this, and enough purification of intelligence and intuition to bring about the discovery we need.

Elsewhere I have told about two men whom I met just after they had come to India. When I asked them why they had come, they said, "We are looking for a qualified guru." And they were taken aback when I responded, "But are you qualified to be disciples of a qualified guru?" That did not please them. When I met them some months later they told me that they had been getting initiated by every guru they met. "Just to be sure" was their answer when I asked them why they were doing such a thing. You might be interested to know that when I first met them I took them to meet Anandamayi Ma whose ashram was only twenty minutes' walk from where they were staying. After about an hour they announced they had to go back for lunch. "Well, you know the way back here," I told them. Their response was, "Oh, it's too far to come back again." But they travelled hundred of miles to collect their initiations from irresponsible gurus. Water found its own level.

Back to Lalla's question. It has no intelligent answer because you cannot name the Unnameable or define the Indefinable. So the question has no value except that when asked it can be answered by what I have just said. There are those who try to increase the scope of their mind, and there are those who try to shrink reality down to their level in the hope of exploiting and controlling it and making it ego-safe. There is a genuine quest for increased understanding, but there is an ego-based fraud that seeks to justify its limitation with the "need to understand," which really means "I will not acknowledge and accept the truth of something I do not like or want to incorporate into my thought and life."

The Nameless Unknown, it seems to me, is the source of the something that we see. That is true. But it must naturally follow that we must consider the possibility that whatever comes from the

Nameless Unknown is the Nameless Unknown Itself. For it is. How can we know if that is true? By becoming an adept yogi.

25.

In life I sought neither wealth nor power,
Nor ran after the pleasures of sense.
Moderate in food and drink, I lived a controlled life,
And loved my God.

This is the formula for success in real life: the path to Self-realization, to the true love of the "God within my breast, almighty, ever-present Deity! Life, that in me has rest, as I, undying Life, have power in Thee!" that was known to Emily Bronte when she also wrote:

> I'm happiest when most away
> I can bear my soul from it's home of clay
> On a windy night when the moon is bright
> And my eye can wander through worlds of light
>
> When I am not and none beside
> Nor earth nor sea nor cloudless sky
> But only spirit wandering wide
> Through infinite immensity.

26.

I came straight,
And straight I shall return.
How can the crooked lead me astray?
Surely, no harm can come to me:
He knows me from the beginning of time,
And loves me.

This is extremely interesting. For the first time Lalla speaks as the Self in each sentient being—the part which is never touched by samsara. She is showing the truth of our inmost being and nature so we can realize that through Soham sadhana we can regain this perspective and free the part of ourselves that is under the spell of maya.

When we are asleep and dreaming that some terrible thing is happening to us we need not resolve or conquer the threat, but simply awake and find it was just a dream. Then all that frightened or pained us is gone and we realize that it never really existed at any time except as an idea and imagination in our mind. The one thing we needed was awakening and seeing that the dream was not reality.

27.

By pandering to your appetites, you get nowhere;
By asceticism and fasting, you get conceit.
Be moderate in food and drink and live a moderate life,
The gates of Heaven will surely be thrown open wide
    for you.

By pandering to your appetites, you get nowhere. "Thinking about sense-objects will attach you to sense-objects; grow attached, and you become addicted; thwart your addiction, it turns to anger; be angry, and you confuse your mind; confuse your mind, you forget the lesson of experience; forget experience, you lose discrimination; lose discrimination, and you miss life's only purpose" (Bhagavad Gita 2:62-63). This is the process within which we lead ourselves astray in this world or relativity which is also illusion. The first time I read it I was deeply impressed. Here was a scripture that told me exactly how my delusive mind works, so I had a chance to stop the folly. And this was in just the second chapter of eighteen! I read on and on, feeling that I was not reading a historical dialogue from long ago, but that my soul was talking to me and telling me the truth. And I wept in profound relief and joy when I came to the final verses:

"Such were the words that thrilled my heart, that marvelous discourse, heard from the lips of the high-souled Prince and the great Lord Krishna. Not with these earthly ears, but by mystic grace of Vyasa, thus I learned that yoga supreme from the Master of yogis. Ever and ever again I rejoice, O King, and remember sacred and wonderful truths that Krishna told to his comrade. Ever again, O King, I am glad and remember rejoicing that most splendid of forms put on by Krishna, the Sweet One. Where Lord Krishna is, and Arjuna, great among archers, there, I know, is goodness and peace, and triumph and glory" (Bhagavad Gita 18:74-78).

Since the senses are oriented toward and filled with the externals of material experience which are essentially a mirage, to live according to the attractions and aversions of the senses and believe that they are real and true, is not only to get nowhere, it is to be nothing. We ourselves become "hungry ghosts" pining after satisfaction through sensory experiences which are ghosts also. It is the state of death, but we can resurrect into life, the life of the spirit. However, we can go about this process in a wrong way.

By asceticism and fasting, you get conceit. Disciplining and denying the body its addictions is a step in the right direction. But since it still is focusing on the material aspects of ourselves, it can lead us into the self-deception that we are being spiritual and following a spiritual life, when we are only taking one of the first steps toward a real spiritual life.

Further, the ego identifies with the body and mind and never with the Self which is its antithesis and its ultimate dissolution. So externalized asceticism feeds the ego and the foolish think they are spiritual if they bend the body to their will through disciplines, especially painful or exaggerated asceticisms. Some are aberrations such as living on milk alone (there was a sadhu in India known as Milk [Dood] Baba, whose only claim to notoriety was having lived on milk for decades), drinking only water taken from the Ganges, eating nothing but neem leaves, extremely prolonged fasting, bathing in every holy river in India on the prescribed days, walking hundreds and thousands of miles to pilgrimage places, and engaging in utterly psychotic practices of self-torture or display. For example there was a man who lived on a pool (billiard) table suspended on ropes for many years, on which he urinated and defecated in plain view, and who was admired because his feces were hard and dry as though baked inside him—something which was cited by his devotees as proof of his inner fires of digestion!

This is no exaggeration or myth. I knew a sadhu who had met this lunatic in his wanderings.

Such insanity is not confined to India but is a part of the "sacred" lore of Buddhism, Taoism, Islam and Christianity.

Be moderate in food and drink and live a moderate life. Few things are more horrible to the ego than being thought ordinary, but it is good for the sensible yogi. Swami Sivananda used to sing:

> Eat a little, drink a little,
> Talk a little, sleep a little,
> Mix a little, move a little,
> Serve a little, rest a little,
> Work a little, relax a little,
> Study a little, reflect a little,...

If you look at videos of Sivananda which show him being visited by various spiritual figures, you will see that most of them have some kind of theatrical "look at holy me" clothing, tilaks (see glossary) and lots of holy beads. Sivananda, however has none of these. It is unfortunate that they came to visit and even honor him, but did not learn from his example of simplicity and modesty.

Of course we must not let our ego fool us into minimal discipline and observance in our spiritual life under the guise of moderation, either. That is a deadly trap, also. I grew up with spiritually lazy and cowardly people who liked to say, "You can go too far" and "You can do too much" in spiritual life. About such people Jesus said, "Verily I say unto you, they have their reward" (Matthew 6:2, 5). And it is very small, I assure you.

The gates of Heaven will surely be thrown open wide for you. Those who are wise enough to be strangers and pilgrims in this world will find their home in the higher worlds where they are living already in their hearts. So they belong there.

28.

Patience to endure lightning and thunder,
Patience to face darkness at noon,
Patience to go through a grinding-mill–
Be patient whatever befalls, doubting not that He will
**   surely come to you.**

Patience is a quality of steadfastness, of the ability to persevere unwaveringly in the face of opposition and distraction. It also implies tranquility of heart even when disruptive elements would impede our steady progress to the goal through Soham sadhana. As the saying goes: a saint is a sinner who never gave up. And considering all that the sadhaka has to endure, the similar saying that a diamond is a piece of coal that never gave up is equally relevant. Intense pressure and intense heat turn coal into diamonds and yogis into siddhas.

Patience to endure lightning and thunder. The ability to remain unmoved and calm in the face of threatening–even frightening–and disruptive situations, persons and inner fears and doubts is the requisite for success in Soham yoga. Negativity both inside and outside us will certainly arise or appear, and we must deal with it by either coming to active grips with it or simply holding tight to our ideals and ignoring it until it passes away and leaves us stronger and wiser in our pursuit of Self-realization.

Patience to face darkness at noon. The "dark night of the soul" leads the sadhaka onward to the full light of spiritual day. Also, to discover that what we thought was light is really darkness, that what we considered truth was actually falsehood, that what (and who) we thought we could relay on for encouragement and support either abandons us or turns on us and tries to deflect us from continuing in the yoga life is a heavy blow. But we must keep moving onward, for in spiritual life there is no standing still. Those who are not going forward are slipping backwards, though they may not realize it.

Patience to go through a grinding-mill. Going through the grinding-mill of life is to have everything go against us and to endure a barrage of opposition and a breaking apart of much that we thought was our support, and to lose much that we have loved, trusted and hoped in—including those we considered closest to us. To be whirled around and ground down unrelentingly is part of the price for the pearl of great price that is total liberation from all bonds. To gain all we must lose all—at least in our willingness to lose all to gain All. There is a hymn that speaks of "feet that have traveled the narrow way, faltering not in the battle fray, treading the thorns in the heat of day." Such are the feet of those who will come at last to the end of the path that leads to divine consciousness.

Be patient whatever befalls, doubting not that He will surely come to you. Or rather, that he will reveal to you that he is there as your inmost being. "The devoted dwell with Him, they know

Him always there in the heart,… they find the place of freedom, the place of no return" (Bhagavad Gita 5:17).

Steady practice of Soham meditation and the observance of the principles of right conduct according to the principles of Sanatana Dharma is the only way to Self-realization. Those who persevere, content in the benefits that Soham meditation gives from the very beginning, will most surely attain the goal of liberation (moksha). This can be the experience of every true and worthy sadhaka-sanatana dharmi. Doubt is dispelled by dharma.

29.

Have no fear, O restless mind,
The Eternal One takes thought for you.
He knows how to fulfil your wants.
Then cry to Him alone for help,
His Name will lead you safe across.

Fearlessness, including complete freedom from anxiety, is a trait of the genuine yogi in the Nath Yogi tradition of Soham sadhana. The way to the Eternal is the path of the Soham yogi. As the great master, Sri Gajanana Maharaj of Nashik, said: "Soham is the sole savior." This, too, is experienced by the devoted Soham sadhaka.

30.

The joys of palate and fine apparel bring man no lasting
  peace.
They who give up false hopes and do not put trust in the
  things of the world,
Ascend, unafraid of Death's terrors by scriptures told;
For having lived contented lives, they are not debtors of
  Desire.
[Alternate translation: And do not have to settle ac-
  counts with the cruel debt-collector Death.]

The joys of palate and fine apparel bring man no lasting peace.
Only those who have realized the futility of centering their
attention and interest in external conditions as the way to inner
happiness and fulfillment and who have understood that there
is no hope of satisfaction and peace in seeking in the things of
earth and ego—and has therefore turned from them and left them
behind—will ascend in consciousness and find that which brings
total fulfillment: Self-realization. "Only that yogi whose joy is
inward, inward his peace, and his vision inward shall come to
Brahman and know Nirvana" (Bhagavad Gita 5:24).

  *They who give up false hopes and do not put trust in the things
of the world,….* Anandamayi Ma often asked people, "Have you
not seen what life in this world is?" For those who see clearly
the truth about this empty and death-bearing material world are
not deceived by the illusions so dear to the hearts of those it has
hypnotized into seeing it in a completely false and unrealistic way.

Ascend, unafraid of Death's terrors by scriptures told. For having lived contented lives, they are not debtors of Desire. [Alternate translation: And do not have to settle accounts with the cruel debt-collector Death.] Fear of death is the great blight and torment of those in this world who are tossed back and forth in the ocean of samsara where there is neither rest nor peace. Our embodied life is only loaned to us for a short time before the karmic forces are exhausted and we lose hold of this life through the death of the body. When the "loan" has been spent, then all is lost which we have fostered and been intent on throughout years and years. In a moment it is gone from our grasp. Young people especially never think of death, but assume they will live forever, even though all around them they see death is an unavoidable fate for every embodied being. What we cling to as life is really nothing more than the prelude to death.

31.

O embodied One, dote not upon your body thus,
Embellishing it, adorning it, providing luxuries for it.
Even its ashes will not endure.

This is the way of true understanding and wisdom. The body is nothing, the spirit within it is everything. Since the body is the container or vehicle of the spirit it is certainly valuable, but its value comes only from its use by the spirit. When the spirit is not the focus of our minds and hearts, then we are utterly worthless even to ourselves. Therefore the wise adorn the spirit and give it comfort, for eventually even the dust of the body will be blown

away and its existence will be totally forgotten, for it will be of
no use to man or God.

32.

Should you, in this body, seek
The Supreme Self that dwells within,
Greed and illusion soon removed,
A halo of glory will surround this very body of yours.

This is a profound and marvelous truth. Throughout the world
in all religions the phenomenon of incorruption of the body after
death has been observed. This is because the spirit, the true Self, when
revealed immortalizes and divinizes even the body, for everything is
ultimately part of The One. I know this to be true, for I have touched
the bodies of living and departed saints in India and America and
experienced the spiritual power they imparted. But that will be of little
use if I do not seek and become one with the Supreme Self.

33.

This counsel to the body give, O Soul:
Wear only such clothes as ward off cold;
Eat only to satisfy your hunger;
Devote yourself with all your heart to the knowledge of
    the Supreme Self.
Consider this body to be food for the forest ravens.

This counsel to the body give, O Soul. The inner being must be
the master and teacher of the outer being. The spirit must become

the instructor and guide of the mind (intelligence). Therefore the wise yogi looks to the Self to be its illumination.

Wear only such clothes as ward off cold. Eat only to satisfy your hunger. This is very difficult for those of us who have passed years of our life being bombarded by the "big is better" and "more is better" philosophy on which an out-of-control and obsessed economy is based. The uncontrolled idea of continual growth and expansion must lead to eventual economic disaster. We have become addicted to Thingism and lose all perspective in the Give Me and I Want race for more, ever more. Fundamental discontent is both the cause and the effect of such an outlook.

In my late teens I met a man who worked in the automobile industry and consequently was forced to join a union which never stopped demanding more money and benefits. Every payday he returned the part of his salary which he considered was overpayment and to accept it was to rob his employer. This completely bewildered everyone involved, but he refused to change his policy. Such a person was rare indeed–he would not sell his soul. But his happy tranquility was a beautiful sight.

Devote yourself with all your heart to the knowledge of the Supreme Self. Consider this body to be food for the forest ravens. [Consider this body meat for jungle crows.] The destiny of the mind (buddhi-intellect) is knowledge-perception of the Self and the yogi's consequent liberation. The destiny of the body is death and decay and destruction in a myriad ways, including being eaten by vultures. So set the mind to work on its destiny and let your body move forward to its destiny. Both are inevitable.

34.

Let not your body suffer from hunger and thirst,
Feed it whenever it feels famished.
Fie on your fasts and religious rites;
Do good: therein your duty lies.

These words show that Lalla, surrounded by the universal insistence on severe asceticism and torture of the body to be a viable spiritual practice, was truly "a voice crying in the wilderness." As the Gita tells us, "Tapasya which is practiced with deluded notions of the Self, and self-torture, is declared to be tamasic [of darkness]" (17:19).

Let not your body suffer from hunger and thirst. Feed it whenever it feels famished. In his autobiography Paramhansa Yogananda said this about his guru, Swami Sriyukteswar Giri: "Master was cautious of his body, while withholding solicitous attachment. The Infinite, he pointed out, properly manifests through physical and mental soundness. He discountenanced any extremes. A disciple once started a long fast. My guru only laughed: 'Why not throw the dog a bone?'"

There was a Zen roshi who worked miracles, much to the delight of his disciples, who boasted of it to a disciple of a non-miraculous roshi. The disciple went to his roshi and told him about it. The roshi smiled and said, "This is my miracle: I eat when I am hungry and I sleep when I am tired." Case closed. The wise yogi does the same. Hunger and thirst are signals that the body needs food and water. What virtue can there be in ignoring the body's innate wisdom? It is the hunger and thirst of the ignorant and deluded mind which we must totally restrain and deny.

Fie on your fasts and religious rites [vratas—vows of abstinence]. Do good: therein your duty lies. And the greatest good—and therefore our greatest duty—is to realize the Self through sadhana. There is no other way.

35.

Do not let loose your donkey-mind
Lest he damage others' saffron fields.
For none will bare his back to suffer
Sword cuts and blows for you.

Do not let loose your donkey-mind lest he damage others' saffron fields. When we let the stupid and lazy donkey-mind roam as it pleases and cause us to do stupid and lazy things instead of wise and spiritually enterprising things, it will damage both our and others' life-fields.

For none will bare his back to suffer sword cuts and blows for you. For no one else will be willing or able to suffer the karma and damage of such neglect but ourselves, and the donkey-mind will suffer as a consequence.

36.

Who slays the highway robbers three, Greed, Lust and
** Pride,**
And yet, in utter humility, serves his fellow-men–
He truly seeks out the Lord,
Disregarding as worthless ashes all other things.

Who slays the highway robbers three, Greed, Lust and Pride....
Those who walk the highway of this world, to which Jesus referred
with the words "broad is the way, that leadeth to destruction,
and many there be which go in thereat" (Matthew 7:13), will be
set upon by three robbers: greed, lust and pride (egotism). They
cannot be simply driven away, for they always return. They have
to be eliminated entirely through diligent Soham sadhana, for
sadhana alone can "slay" them.

And yet, in utter humility, serves his fellow-men.... The service
humanity needs is deliverance from the Three Robbers, so only
those who can show them the way to slay these thieves really serve
others. And each one must slay these enemies himself–neither God
nor his saints will do it for him.

He truly seeks out the Lord, disregarding as worthless ashes all
other things. What a beautiful idea, however ugly it may be to the
distorted minds and hearts of those who love and seek the world
and its ways, for "the friendship of the world is enmity with God.
Whosoever therefore will be a friend of the world is the enemy of
God" (James 4:4). To seek God above all and to consider all else
as worthless ashes is the way to gain the wealth of Life Eternal.
We need not waste our time "hating" or "despising" the world, for

that would be to fix our minds on the world. Rather, we ignore the ways of the world as the lying mirages they are and seek for the only truth: Self-realization.

37.

Slay the murderous demons, Lust, Anger and Greed;
Or, aiming their arrows at you, they will surely shoot you dead.
Take care, feed them on self-restraint and discrimination of the Self.
Thus starved these demons will become powerless and weak.

Slay the murderous demons, Lust [Kama], Anger [Krodha] and Greed [Lobha]. Kama is desire, passion and lust; krodha is anger, wrath, and fury; and lobha is greed and covetousness. They kill those who harbor or tolerate them in any way. Once they have arrived they cannot be driven away, they can only be slain.

Or, aiming their arrows at you, they will surely shoot you dead. There is no compromise with such enemies!

Take care, feed them on self-restraint and discrimination of the Self. When these evil impulses arise, counter ("feed") them with the discipline of self-restraint and the wisdom of the discrimination of the Self from the not-self and all that wars against the realization of the Self. Do not fight them or "touch" them in any manner. "Feed" them the salutary remedy of Soham sadhana and you will be healed and they will be dissolved or transmuted into spiritual vigor.

Thus starved these demons will become powerless and weak. Experience the truth of this for yourself through Soham sadhana.

38.

They may abuse me or jeer at me,
They may say what pleases them,
They may with flowers worship me.
What profits them whatever they do?
I am indifferent to praise and blame.

This is an expression of what has been called Holy Indifference, meaning that when someone is immersed in the consciousness of his true nature as the Self, nothing moves or distracts him. "He rests in the inner calm of the Atman, regarding happiness and suffering as one.... He pays no attention to praise or to blame. His behavior is the same when he is honored and when he is insulted" (Bhagavad Gita 14:24-25). For when the yogi possesses and unbrokenly lives in the consciousness of the Self nothing else matters. When I was young I often sang a song with the refrain:

> That wicked one toucheth him not,
> That wicked one toucheth him not;
> He keepeth himself in the love of the Lord,
> And that wicked one toucheth him not.

After reading the Gita and becoming a yogi I really knew the meaning of these words. For it says:

"Seek refuge in the knowledge of Brahman" (Bhagavad Gita 2:49).

"Burnt clean in the blaze of my being, in me many find home" (Bhagavad Gita 4:10).

"Devote your whole mind to me, and practice yoga. Take me for your only refuge" (Bhagavad Gita 7:1).

"He who takes refuge within me only shall pass beyond Maya: he, and no other" (Bhagavad Gita 7:14).

"Know me to be your only refuge. Be united always in heart and consciousness with me" (Bhagavad Gita 18:57)

"The Lord lives in the heart of every creature.... Take refuge utterly in him. By his grace you will find supreme peace, and the state which is beyond all change" (Bhagavad Gita 18:61-62).

39.

Let them mock at me and call me names.
If a true devotee of Shiva I be,
I shall not feel distressed nor hurt.
Can a few ashes a mirror befoul?

Whatever the external insults or misfortunes may be, those who are devoted to the Shiva-Self that alone is real and true will not be disturbed even in their inmost being. Not identifying with the ego and its mayic personality, the yogi cannot be shaken or altered in any way, just as a silver mirror cannot be dirtied by a few ashes falling on it. Just a puff of the breath and the mirror is as before. In the same way, just the reorientation of the mind through japa and meditation of Soham will restore everything about the yogi to its original purity and right order.

40.

Though you are wise, be as a fool;

Though you can see, be as one blind;

Though you can hear, be as one deaf;

Patiently bear with all you meet, and politely talk to everyone.

This practice surely will lead you to the realization of the Truth.

Three times in the Bhagavad Gita the yogi is advised to live a solitary life.

"The yogi should retire into a solitary place, and live alone" (6:10).

"Turn all your thought toward solitude, spurning the noise of the crowd, its fruitless commotion" (Bhagavad Gita 13:10).

"When a man seeks solitude,… that man is ready for oneness with Brahman" (Bhagavad Gita 18:52-53).

This does not mean that he should be anti-social, but definitely he should be non-social to a marked degree, for he must be independent in mind and self-sufficient. Those who are continually socializing become externalized, influenced by and even made dependent on others, often drawing their self-image from their associates. "People who need people" are truly the most unfortunate, weak and dependent people in the world, lacking self-reliance, self-respect and self-awareness.

Therefore Lalla tells the aspiring yogi to keep aloof from people, and when he cannot avoid being with them to be as though he were a blockhead–to not react to or be drawn into worldly conversation with them and become a part of their samsara-oriented and dominated ways. This is not snobbish; it is the way of the wise. Whenever Swami Sriyukteswar Giri, Yogananda's guru, instructed someone in yoga meditation he would ask them if they knew anyone who was a yogi. If they replied that they did, he would tell them: "Good. Make them your only friends."

Naturally, what I am saying does not mean a yogi should sever ties with his close family members and certainly not with his spouse and children. But with others it is good to be aloof. And they will usually separate themselves–just disappear.

One of my first yoga students who had many social attachments several times said to me: "It isn't good to hurt anyone's feelings, is it?" This was because he had many friends whose ways were utterly incompatible with the yoga life, the type about whom Jesus was speaking when he told his disciples about those who would demand from them conformity to their ways: "Whereunto then shall I liken the men of this generation? and to what are they like? They are like unto children sitting in the marketplace, and calling one to another, and saying, We have piped unto you, and ye have not danced; we have mourned to you, and ye have not wept" (Luke 7:31-32.) About such people Saint Peter wrote: "They think it strange that ye run not with them to the same excess of riot, speaking evil of you" (I Peter 4:4). I told him, "Meditate and elevate your consciousness and you will go out of their world and they will forget you even exist." He did not believe me, but he did meditate—and they did forget his existence, never once contacting him after he became a yogi. This is the way of the world, to which we should be "strangers and pilgrims" (Hebrews 11:13; I Peter 2:11).

41.

The ocean and the mind of man are both alike:

Under the ocean's bottom lies the destructive fire, vadvaagni;

And in the breast of man doth rage the fire of wrath.

When the fire breaks out, its flames of angry, abusive words, sear and scorch and burn.

But if one ponders unruffled and calm, and weighs the words, though angry they be,

They have no substance, no, nor weight.

The ocean and the mind of man are both alike: under the ocean's bottom lies the destructive fire, vadvagni; and in the breast of man doth rage the fire of wrath. It is said in the ancient scriptures of India that there is beneath the ocean floor a terrible form of fire, vadvagni, which would destroy the whole world it it were to burst forth from under the ocean.

When the fire breaks out, its flames of angry, abusive words, sear and scorch and burn. The mind itself is a potential fire, wounding both us and all around us if we let it go unchecked. It is a wild thing that needs taming, Soham yoga being the best means to tame it.

But if one ponders unruffled and calm, and weighs the words, though angry they be, they have no substance, no, nor weight. If we calmly weigh the words and ways of the samsaric mind in the experience of the divine Self, then all the other words and ways of illusion and delusion are seen as worthless, "weighing" nothing morally speaking. They are nonsense, but poisonous nonsense that leads us astray. Soham sadhana is the scale in which we should weigh all things.

42.

Ill or well, whatever befalls, let it come.
My ears will not hear, my eyes will not see.
When the Voice calls from within the inmost mind,
The lamp of faith burns steady and bright even in the
    wind.

Ill or well, whatever befalls, let it come. Whatever comes to us in life is nothing but the force of our own karmas, positive and negative. Their coming is an absolute destiny, there is no way around it. So we need to adopt the motto: Ill or well, whatever befalls, let it come. For come it will. Nothing can prevent or hold it back.

My ears will not hear, my eyes will not see. That is, my mind will not respond or react to what is heard or seen. But it will remain in the calm of the Self.

When the Voice calls from within the inmost mind, the lamp of faith burns steady and bright even in the wind. When through Soham sadhana the inner Voice is heard (experienced) arising directly from the Self, the resulting clarity and illumination of mind will not be shaken or dimmed by any outside experience or force.

43.

When can I break the bonds of shame?
When I am indifferent to jibes and jeers.
When can I discard the robe of dignity?
When desires cease to nag my mind.

When can I break the bonds of shame? When I am indifferent to jibes and jeers. I have never known the "sticks and stones" platitude to work. That is because it is an intellectual concept which never touches the emotions of the offended or wounded ego or leads to the inmost Self. The way to become indifferent to either praise or blame, admiration or mockery, is to know who/what we really are: the Self. Then external opinion means nothing: we know what we are and what we are not. The secret is establishment in our core being, described by the Gita as "he whose happiness is within, whose delight is within, whose illumination is within" (5:24), "contented in the Self by the Self" (2:55), "content only in the Self, who is satisfied in the Self, who is pleased only in the Self" (3:17), "absorbed in the Self alone, with mind controlled, free from longing, from all desires" (6:18), and "restrained by the practice of yoga, beholding the Self by the Self, he is content in the Self" (6:20). "As a lamp in a windless place flickers not: to such is compared the yogi of controlled mind, performing the yoga of the Self" (6:19).

When can I discard the robe of dignity? When desires cease to nag my mind. One of the noble delusions of the ego is the insistence on "self-respect," "self-worth" and "self-confidence" which cloaks the desire for personal attainment and gaining the high opinion of others.

When the fire of desire is extinguished in relation to ourselves we will experience the description Krishna gives of the wise in the Gita: "His attitude is the same toward friend and foe. He is indifferent to honor and insult, heat and cold, pleasure and pain. He is free from attachment" (Bhagavad Gita 12:18). Disillusionment and disappointment can create a false and momentary detachment, but since it is unreal nothing positive results from it. But the yogi knows that the fire of desire is put out by resting in his own Self. "What God's Will gives he takes, and is contented. Pain follows pleasure, he is not troubled: gain follows loss, he is indifferent: of whom should he be jealous? He acts, and is not bound by his action" (Bhagavad Gita 4:22).

44.

I have worn out my palate and tongue reading the holy
    books,
But I have not learnt the practices that would please my
    Lord.
I have worn thin my finger and thumb telling the rosary
    beads,
But I have not been able to dispel duality from my mind.

Duality cannot be dispelled from the mind because the things listed are based on duality and affirm it by their very nature. We read scriptures to supposedly find out the mind and will of God. We "do good" in order to please God. We wear out ourselves banging away at mantras whose object is separate from us and therefore an entrenchment in dualistic consciousness. Since God and the sadhaka are essentially one, though not essentially the same, only that which affirms and reveals that unity is worthwhile or even real. The real sacred truth of unity is not found in scriptures, nor in "doing good" and attempting to "please" God. It is not in fixing the mind on external "deities" by mantras that assume duality and not unity. Only one thing solves Lalla's dilemma: the realization of Soham–I Am That–through Soham Yoga.

45.

It is easy to read and to recite;
It is hard to practice what one reads,
And, reading seek out the Self within.
By constant practice, not by books,
Conviction grew in my heart
Of God, Who is Consciousness-Bliss.

It is easy to read and to recite; it is hard to practice what one reads, and, reading seek out the Self within. It is not only hard for the samsaric mind–it is distasteful and offensive. The effort required to realize God is very small compared to the effort that human beings put forth to evade God and exalt their egos and desires.

By constant practice, not by books, conviction grew in my heart of God, Who is Consciousness-Bliss. Sadhana–Soham sadhana–alone establishes us in the knowledge of Satchidananda: Existence-Knowledge-Bliss Absolute.

47.

I practiced what I read, and learnt what was not taught.
From its jungle abode I brought the lion down as I,
a jackal would;
From pleasures of the world I pulled my mind away.
I practiced what I preached, and scored the goal.

The true scriptures are based on the realities of God and the individual Self. They exhort us to seek the reality of ourself which is God. Those who do this learn far more than the books contain, for scriptures are only hints. Real yoga is the journey of discovery of the Infinite. It is going into the jungle of the mind and slaying the lion of ego and illusion. Then separation from attraction to the ways of the world can be accomplished, and living as though God is real through yoga will guarantee our liberation into Spirit.

48.

You will not know peace of mind if you a kingdom gain,
Nor will you gain content or rest if you give it away.
Only the man, free from desire, will never die.
Only he has true knowledge
Who, though alive, is as one dead, dead to all desire.

You will not know peace of mind if you a kingdom gain. Just the opposite: the duties and anxieties of ruling an entire kingdom will ensure that you will have no rest and no peace. So to desire a kingdom is to desire measureless discontent and frustration. Being a king means nothing if no one pays attention to him or even recognizes him as king. He will have to keep asserting himself again and again without any respite.

Nor will you gain content or rest if you give it away. This is because the mind will not let it go. And watching another make mistakes in ruling will create the desire to reclaim it and rule according to your ideas. And then you will be back where you started. Unhappy with a kingdom and unhappy without a kingdom. The mind will not let go whatever the outer conditions may be.

Only the man, free from desire, will never die. I remember an architect friend of our monastery that once went with us to look at a house we might have a use for. As we walked away from viewing it, she said with real fervor: "My mother would have died a thousand deaths if she had seen that house!" So to die is much more than losing the body. Every disappointment, failure and frustration is a personal death. As long as desire is present this will be the case, whether we are a beggar or an emperor. To desire nothing is to have everything, for desire comes from a feeling of need or deficiency which can never really be satisfied–or only temporarily. As the Bhagavad Gita says: "Renunciation brings instant peace to the spirit" (12:12). Of such a one the Gita further says: "He does not desire or rejoice in what is pleasant. He does not dread what is unpleasant, or grieve over it. He remains unmoved by good or evil fortune" (Bhagavad Gita 12:17). "He knows peace who has forgotten desire. He lives without craving: free from ego, free from pride" (Bhagavad Gita 2:71).

Only he has true knowledge who, though alive, is as one dead, dead to all desire. This seems contradictory to the previous statement, but it is based on a different meaning of "death." This sentence is saying that if while the samsaric individual is "alive" to samsara it can transfer its awareness into its real nature of spirit-consciousness and "die to the world" it will attain true knowledge and come to know its true Self. Therefore Saint Paul wrote: " I die daily" (I Corinthians 15:31).

49.

**I have to suffer the consequence of whatever I do, even
    if I work for others' gain.**
**But if, with mind from attachment free, I dedicate all
    works to God,**
It will be well for me wherever I be, here and hereafter.

I have to suffer the consequence of whatever I do, even if I work for others' gain. For every action there is an equal and opposite reaction. This is not Newton's Law, it is divine law. Therefore, however unselfish and altruistic an action may be, still karma accrues to the one doing the action. I have no idea why Lalla felt this needed to be said, but perhaps at that time some noble sentimentalist was claiming that noble deeds produced no karmic seeds. Anyhow: they do.

But if, with mind from attachment free, I dedicate all works to God, it will be well for me wherever I be, here and hereafter. For action in relation to God–including seeing or considering those involved in the action as essentially divine–becomes divine karma, a force for the ultimate Self-realization of the yogi.

50.

Why do you grope thus like the blind?
Pray, doubt not what I say to you:
If you are wise, enter within
And see the Lord Himself is there.
You need not search Him here and there.

Those who do not see with the inner eye of spiritual consciousness are blind, and their entire life is only groping in the darkness. But the wise heed the counsel of the enlightened and become, like them, established in the inmost awareness of the Self. For God is neither "here" nor "there" but within each one of us. When we find and know our own Self then we will find and know the Self of our Self—Brahman the Absolute.

51.

He who can direct his prana aright, is not troubled by hunger or thirst.
And he who can do this unto the end is born fortunate in this world.

He who can direct his prana aright, is not troubled by hunger or thirst. This has three meanings, all of which I am sure Lalla intended. First, thinking of prana as life, there is the principle that those who orient their life toward the highest consciousness will never hunger or thirst in their inmost being, for "Blessed are they which do hunger and thirst after righteousness: for they shall be filled" (Matthew 5:6). Second, those who can direct their pranic life force into the higher levels and centers of awareness within will likewise not hunger and thirst, having been "filled" with Life Itself. Third, those who direct their breath aright by joining the mantra Soham to it as mentioned before, will certainly become untroubled even in the midst of external troubles. Such is the yogi.

And he who can do this unto the end is born fortunate in this world. His life here has been fruitful. For "he that endureth to the end shall be saved" (Matthew 10:22) through the attainment of liberation: moksha.

52.

The steed of mind speedeth over the sky.
And, in the twinkling of the eye,
A hundred thousand leagues traverseth he.
Yet a man of discrimination can control the curvetting
    steed,
And, on the wheels of prana and apana, guide his char-
    iot aright.

The steed of mind speedeth over the sky. The chitta is the subtle energy that is the substance of the mind, and therefore the higher mind, the field of consciousness itself. It moves in the chidakasha, the expanse of the subtle etheric realm, like lightning. One of its common movements is the leap or flash of intuition.

And, in the twinkling of the eye, a hundred thousand leagues traverseth he. Through illumined intuition, to the inner eye of the yogi measureless distance is traversed in a moment.

Yet a man of discrimination can control the curvetting steed, and, on the wheels of prana and apana, guide his chariot aright. The adept yogi knows how to tame the movements of his outer and inner life forces, to direct them into the inner sky or space and establish them there by yogic processes and thus into the pure, limitless consciousness of the Self.

As he seizes the horse by the bridle of self-realization. Although secondary processes affect the secondary aspects of our being, the chitta is fully tamed and corralled only through Self-realization. Then all movement is at an end and only pure awareness of the Self remains. Soham yoga sadhana alone accomplishes this.

53.

Keep your mind intent upon the path that leads to im-
    mortality.
Should it stray from the path, it will fall into evil ways.
Be firm with it and have no fear;
For the mind is like a suckling baby, which tosses restless
    even in its mother's lap.

Keep your mind intent upon the path that leads to immortality. For Lalla the path that leads to immortality was the japa and meditation of Soham. Whatever the activity, the serious yogi does his utmost to keep the inner repetition/experience of the Soham mantra in his awareness at all times. It is worth the effort, as you can discover for yourself.

Should it stray from the path, it will fall into evil ways. The mind devoid of the presence of the Soham mantra will certainly stray into evil ways. Not terrible crimes or hideously evil thoughts, but the "death" of a consciousness devoid of the divinizing presence of Soham in the awareness.

Two of my Indian friends upon their retirement went to live in the holy city of Haridwar where there was an ashram for married couples. Though accustomed to wealth and luxury, they lived in an apartment of two small rooms–one of them being living room, kitchen and dining room combined. On the wall of this room was a framed motto: I REMEMBER RAM AND I LIVE. I FORGET RAM AND I DIE.

It is the same with Soham. To remember its invocation is to live and increase our life, but to forget it is to lapse in the half-life we lived before we learned of it.

Be firm with it and have no fear; for the mind is like a suckling baby, which tosses restless even in its mother's lap. A baby often crawls around getting into things and trouble. The mother, involved in her work, yet has to keep bringing it back into safe territory. Although we wish our minds did not stray and lose hold of Soham, they will anyway. So we keep bringing them back to where they belong–in Soham awareness. "No matter where the restless and the unquiet mind wanders, it must be drawn back" (Bhagavad Gita 6:26). For just as it is the nature of the baby to be restless even in its mother's lap, it is the nature of the mind to wander away from or be distracted from Soham, even though Soham is the very essence of the yogi's consciousness and life.

54.

Who dies? Who is slain?
He who forsakes God's Name,
And gets involved in worldly cares.
It is he who dies. It is he who is slain.

This certainly needs no comment, but it needs to be taken to heart and kept in mind. Speaking of Soham japa and meditation, Sri Gajanana Maharaj of Nashik said the following (from *Light of Soham*): "My sadguru had me drink the nectar [amrita] of Nama [Name of God] and I tell you the same Nama, being ordered by my sadguru to do so. I am approaching the stage of perfection. If you also wish to come with me, you should repeat that Nama, Soham, in your heart with firm faith. One must remember that the Siddha Name of Soham alone will be useful in easily crossing this ocean of worldly existence and ending the cycle of births and deaths. This Siddha Nama is a power; it is like a mother to the universe, and it is the entity that is calling itself 'I' in the body. It is a flame of love."

Most words, even names, are designations—nothing more. But Soham is different, for as Gajanana Maharaj further said, "He who makes that Nama his own becomes one with the universal power. His words acquire the force of truth, and hence are full of power." This can be the experience of anyone who applies himself to Soham Yoga.

55.

He who has faith in Guru's word,
And with true knowledge for the rein
Guides aright the steed of mind,
And holds his senses in control,
'Tis he enjoys the peace of mind.
He will not die, nor be slain.

Lalla has given us here the formula for immortality: faith in
the words of the spiritual teacher and the true knowledge that
comes from the following of those words which include the perfect
control of those elements in our makeup that tend to run away
and create havoc in the runaway mind that carries us into peril
over and over by its instability and weakness. The Gita has the
following verses about the mind that should be taken very seriously.

"A serene spirit accepts pleasure and pain with an even mind,
and is unmoved by either. He alone is worthy of immortality"
(Bhagavad Gita 2:15). "Even a mind that knows the path can be
dragged from the path: the senses are so unruly. But he [the yogi]
controls the senses and recollects the mind" (Bhagavad Gita 2:60-
61). "The wind turns a ship from its course upon the waters: the
wandering winds of the senses cast man's mind adrift and turn his
better judgment from its course. When a man can still the senses I
call him illumined. The recollected mind is awake in the knowledge
of the Atman" (Bhagavad Gita 2:67-69). "The senses are said to be
higher than the sense-objects. The mind is higher than the senses.
The intelligent will is higher than the mind. What is higher than
the intelligent will? The Atman Itself. You must know Him who

is above the intelligent will. Get control of the mind" (Bhagavad Gita 3:42-43).

Lalla and the Gita do not tell us to pray to God and ask him to do all these things for us. Knowledge that does not show us how to do these things is not knowledge in the highest sense at all. "This true wisdom I have taught will lead you to immortality. The faithful practice it with devotion, taking me for their highest aim" (Bhagavad Gita 12:20).

56.

Sure and steady the mill will turn once you propel the
　　wheel.
Mind is the pivot, it should know how best to turn the mill.
And once it turns, it will grind fine,
And grain will find its way to the mill.

Reality is beyond the lower mind of mere intellect, but the highest faculty of the mind, intuition developed through yoga meditation, rises and comes to see the way. Such a "mill" grinds the seed-grains of karmic force coming from our past actions and thoughts (samskaras) and ensures they will never sprout and manifest in our minds or in our lives. The mind learns "how best to turn the mill" through the practice of meditation.

57.

Shiva abides in all that is, everywhere;
Then do not discriminate between a Hindu or a Mus-
salman.
If thou art wise, know thyself;
That is true knowledge of the Lord.

This is not about considering all religions equal. It is about social discrimination between the adherents of differing religions. Both Hindus and Moslems liked to give each other derogatory names and to treat each other like unclean and untouchable beings. Very cruel words and deeds resulted, each blaming the other for the problem. The spiritually wise on both sides tried to rid their fellow religionists of this prejudice and hatred, but that usually resulted in their own side turning against and rejecting them, too! So Lalla counsels them to forget reforming the ignorant and put all their energy into gaining Self-knowledge, and thus coming to know God as a consequence. There never is much use in trying to reform others, but reforming ourselves is possible–especially if we are yogis.

58.

I taught my mind to see the One in all my fellow-men.
How could I then discriminate between man and man,
And not accept the food offered to me by brother man?

Being greedy, the "don't touch me" Hindus and Moslems usually displayed their prejudice in matters of food and drink, refusing to eat or drink anything touched by the other side as being polluted and polluting. Faced with this attitude himself, Guru Nanak wanted to spend his inheritance on building both temples and mosques, but the Hindus and Moslems howled at the thought and threatened him if he should do such a thing. So he spent the money on building public toilets instead. "They can both understand and appreciate those," he commented. And they did.

59.

O fool, right action does not lie in observing fasts and ceremonial rites.

O fool, right action does not lie in providing for bodily comfort and ease.

In contemplation of the Self alone is right action and right counsel for you.

This is quite clear. The only real and true right action is meditation and living out its resulting insight.

60-61.

First feed the Five Bhutas on the grain and delicacies of Self-awareness;

Thus fed, offer these fatted rams as sacrifice unto the Lord.

Then you will know, O restless one, the abode of the Supreme.

Ceremonial rites and pieties will cease to be binding on you;

And even the left-handed practices will bring no harm to you.

Each one of us lives in the world of five elements–earth, water, fire, air and ether. And we also possess five bodies formed from them–the physical/material, pranic, mental, intellect and intuitional bodies: annamaya, pranamaya, manomaya, jnanamaya and anandamaya koshas. We should feed all five of them on Self-knowledge (Atmajnana) drawn from yoga sadhana. Then they will be fit offerings unto God.

When we then come to know ourselves as the highest temples of the Divine, external religious observances will cease to mean much if anything to us. And any actions, even if "left-handed" in the sense of wrongly or defectively done, will only bring us good, not harm.

(Some think that "left-handed" refers to left-hand Tantric practices that will not harm the sadhaka even if worked against him. It positively does not mean that the sadhaka can engage in such practices and not come to harm. No one can perform evil or unclean deeds and not create and suffer the negative consequences.)

62.

The pathway of jnana is a vegetable garden;
Fence it with self-restraint and pious deeds.
Then let the goats of former karma browse in it
And fattened be as animals fit for sacrifice at the altar of
the Mother.

True jnana is possible of attainment only to the yogi. It has nothing to do with empty scholarship and equally empty philosophy. It is a path of yoga sadhana. When yama-niyama are observed and the righteous life lived, the "goats of former karma" become ready for the "sacrifice" of annihilation at the hands of the Cosmic Mother, Mahashakti. Jai Ma.

63.

Who can stop the eaves' drip during the frost?
Who can hold wind in the palm of his hand?
Who can see the sun in the darkness of night?
He who holds his senses under control,
Can in the dark catch hold of the sun.

The yoga siddha alone can do all these things through intense sadhana that reveals his Self. Such a one literally seizes and enters into the blazing sun of the Self.

"The Atman is the light: the light is covered by darkness: this darkness is delusion... When the light of the Atman drives out our darkness that light shines forth from us, a sun in splendor, the revealed Brahman" (Bhagavad Gita 5:15-16).

"By the single sun this whole world is illumined: by its one Knower [the Atman] the Field is illumined" (Bhagavad Gita 13:33).

"Flying from fear, from lust and anger, he hides in me his refuge, his safety: burnt clean in the blaze of my being, in me many find home" (Bhagavad Gita 4:10).

64.

Like water in a colander are name and fame: they do
 not last.
Whoever in his fist can hold a storm,
Or tether an elephant with a hair of his head,
'Tis he whose name and fame endure.

A sieve will let out the water the moment it is poured into
it. There is no grasping or holding on to it possible. It is gone in
a moment as though it were never there. So is the respect and
honor of this world. They evaporate eventually, and disrespect and
dishonor often take their places. So the liking and respect of the
world and the worldly are doomed to annihilation, but disrespect
and dishonor can live for a long time, even centuries. As Napoleon
said, "History is a lie agreed upon." This is usually true. The lesson
in this verse is to be indifferent to the praise and blandishments
of this world and move on secure in our own integrity, knowing
ourselves as what we really are: the Self.

We cannot grasp the wind or bind an elephant with one hair of
our head. Therefore lasting "success" in this world means nothing.
It is just a mirage like the world itself. The wise turn within and
find the real everlasting life. "Only that yogi whose joy is inward,
inward his peace, and his vision inward shall come to Brahman
and know Nirvana" (Bhagavad Gita 5:24). "Then he knows that
infinite happiness which can be realized by the purified heart but
is beyond the grasp of the senses. He stands firm in this realization.
Because of it, he can never again wander from the inmost truth
of his being" (Bhagavad Gita 6:21).

This is the only goal worth seeking.

65.

It covers your shame,
Saves you from cold,
Its food and drink–
Mere water and grass.
Who counseled you, O brahmin,
To slaughter a living sheep as a sacrifice
Unto a lifeless stone?

It seems to be the nature of human beings to sink into degradation and take their religion along with them. And since the killing of animals, eating their flesh and wearing their skins is an act of utmost degradation, their religion engages in animal sacrifice. Apparently harmless sheep were favorite victims at the time of Lalla, who lists all the benefits given to humanity by the sheep which would be killed to placate a lifeless stone image in an equally degraded temple.

66.

The idol is but stone,
The temple is but stone,
From top to bottom all is stone.
Whom will you worship, O learned Pandit?
Let prana and the mind unite (as an offering to your
    God).

We must not mistakenly think that Lalla is propounding the mistaken idea that an image is only stone, so is the temple, and therefore only stone is being worshipped—and not God. (I well remember how annoyed I was when an ignorant Indian Christian said to one of the monks of our ashram regarding Hindus: "They worship a stone." Not so!)

However, if a priest (pujari) or worshipper is not a yogi and therefore sees only stone, then he does only worship stone. But Lalla gives the solution to such persons:

Uniting the pranas, the subtle life forces which comprise our various bodies, with our focused mind (chitta) through Soham yoga sadhana, we will begin to see truly with the "eye" of the spirit-Self and therefore perceive that everything is consciousness and not "dead matter" as we presently think and therefore experience. It is like the parable of the blind men who had all kinds of opinions on the nature of an elephant when only a person with eyesight could really see and know the nature of the elephant.

Those who are blinded by ignorance (maya) understand nothing of reality, outer and inner. But those who are awake in their total being can truthfully say with Swami Sivananda's poem: "Only God I Saw." When people who thought themselves jnanis—enlightened non-dual philosophers—would complain to Anandamayi Ma about image worship as idolatry she would simply tell them: "You must come to see the Divine Consciousness within the image." The problem was in their limited awareness.

"Therefore be a yogi" (Bhagavad Gita 6:46). True sacrifice is the diligent practice of sadhana in which the life forces and the mind unite as one and merge with the Self as the only fit offering to the Absolute.

67.

> He does not need the kusha grass, nor sesame seed;
> Flowers and water He does not need.
> He who, in honest faith, accepts his Guru's word,
> On Shiva meditates constantly, His is the true worship
>   of the Lord.
> He, full of joy, from action freed, will not be born again.

All the paraphernalia of ritualistic worship are not needed by the yogi. (Notice that Lalla does not denigrate them in relation to the non-yogi who can only worship with such items.)

He who has been shown the yogic path and follows it by the constant fixing of his consciousness on the Infinite through continual japa and meditation of Soham, is thereby made "full of joy, from action freed, [and] will not be born again." This is the true religion.

68-69.

Who is the florist, who the flower-girl?
With what flowers should He be worshipped?
In what water should He be bathed?
With what mantra should we awaken Shankara,
Who abides in the Self?
Mind is the florist, devotion the flower-girl,
who bring flower-wreaths for Him.
He should be worshipped with the flowers of faith,
And bathed in the nectar of the Mystic Moon.
Silence is the mantra that awakens Him.

The external, material objects so prized for ritualistic worship in homes and temples accomplish absolutely nothing for the awakening of the Self in the practice of yoga, the only true worship and religion. Faith and union with the yogi's Self which is the reflection of the Supreme Self and which is beyond all words is the Shiva-Self which must be awakened.

70.

Thou art the earth, Thou art the sky,
Thou art the air, the day and the night;
The sacrificial grain Thou,
And anointing with the sandal-paste.
Thou art the water, Thou art the flowers,
Thou art all these and everything.
What may I, in worship, bring to Thee?

Only our Self, purified and illumined by perfection in yoga.

71.

He who knows the Dvadashaanta Mandala as the abode
  of God,

And knows the constant Sound that is borne upon the
  prana rising from the heart to the nose,

All vain imaginings flee from his mind, without effort,
  naturally;

He knows no God other than the Self, nor need he worship any other god.

The dvadashanta mandala (yantra) is a diagram engraved on
a metal plate or formed by auspicious elements on a plate before
or on which ritualistic worship of a deity is performed.

The Sound is the ajapa japa mantra of Soham.

Those who know that both are essentially the Self of the yogi
and therefore continually fix their minds on the mantra Soham
will find that all worthless things depart from their thoughts spontaneously–though this does take some time of practice! Soham
Bhava, the essence of his own Self embodied in the mantra Soham,
is the only deity the yogi can either worship or know.

72.

He in whose inmost being constantly abides none other
    than the eternal Soham,
Who builds a bridge between his own [consciousness]
    and Cosmic Consciousness,
By making his mind one with this mighty mantra–
What need has he for a thousand other mantras?

Here we have the complete picture. Soham is already the inmost
being or essence of the yogi. Soham sadhana "builds a bridge between
his own and Cosmic Consciousness, by making his mind [conscious-
ness] one with this mighty mantra." What purpose could any other
mantra have for him? Soham Kevalam: Soham Alone.

73.

Shiva or Keshava or Jina,
Or Brahma, the lotus-born Lord,
Whatever name He bear,
May He remove from me
The sickness of the world!
It may be He or He or He
(For He is One though called variously).

There are literally thousands of designative and descriptive
names of God the Nameless and Unnameable. Here Lalla is saying
that God may be thought of in the context of Shaivism (worship
of Shiva), Vaishnavism (worship of Vishnu or his avatars), Jainism,
or Hinduism in general. But the prayer of the wise among them

all is this: "May He remove from me the sickness of the world!" Continual rebirth in relative existence, and especially in this world of constant birth and death, is the samsara (life through repeated births and deaths; the process of earthly life) that is truly a disease—a plague, rather. Suffering of mind and body is the keynote of the entire situation, based on confusion and ignorance of our true Self. From life to life we have no idea how or why we are here, or even what "here" really is. The ocean of samsara casts us up perpetually on the shore of birth and then takes us away with the tide of death. Over and over this happens to us, and we in our insanity both suffer from it and yet long for it, fearing that if it ends our existence will end.

Part of the answer to our sickness is to become through wisdom "sick of the world" and strive to cure ourselves and get released from the "contagious ward" that is the world. When Yogananda was creating the Lake Shrine in Pacific Palisades many residents of the ashram worked there. One morning a boy who was living there with his mother and going to school daily, expressed his wish to Yogananda that he could go and do some work at the Lake Shrine. "Call up the school and tell them you are sick," replied Yogananda. "But I am not sick," protested the boy. "Yes, you are," said Yogananda, "You are sick of the world." A blessed sickness, indeed!

Whatever name or title or concept of God we may hold, it does not matter. May he heal us of the disease of bondage in and to this world and liberate our Self from all the illusory bonds that do not even really bind it!

74.

I, Lalla, searched and sought for Him, and even beyond
    my strength I strove.
Finding His doors bolted and barred I longed the more;
And firmly resolved, I stood just there with longing and
    love,
Fixing my gaze upon His door.

75.

In the mortar of love I ground my heart,
I parched and burnt and ate it out.
Thus, all my evil passions removed,
I sat serene and unperturbed.
Yet still I doubt if I can know
Whether I shall die or I shall live.

76.

Not by ascetic practices is the Self realized;
Nor by desire can you gain the Portals of Release.
In contemplation you may be absorbed as salt in water,
Yet hard it is for you to gain the true knowledge of the
    Self.

Even over-reaching our strength and will cannot by its limited
nature open the doors to liberation into the Absolute. So Lalla
"stood just there with longing and love, fixing my gaze upon
His door." And seeming non-doing was the most potent action,

for it was the total fixing of the will power upon the portal of Self-realization.

Lalla burnt up and ground to powder her heart–the deep inner mind, the very bhava of her existence. But although all passions dissolved and she attained undisturbed inner tranquillity, she could not discern if she would have succeeded in conquering inner, spiritual death and becoming immortal, for ascetic practices cannot reveal the Self, nor can mere desire or yearning (whose value the bhakti school exaggerates to an absurd degree) or seeming profound absorption in meditation. (Once I saw a woman faking such meditation until Anandamayi Ma came up to her and literally shouted in her face to get up and get out! She did. Immediately. But she was later to show up in Brindavan and during morning meditation begin shouting "Jai Ho!" over and over while rolling around on the floor. Ma immediately said that she should be picked up and thrown out of the hall. That was done, and at the end of meditation when Ma came out of the hall she went up to woman who was lying immobile in the blazing sun with closed eyes. Ma gave her a quick look of indifference and walked on.)

Gaining the true knowledge of the Self is a long road and impossible to gain by the fake-or-non-yogi.

77.

Plump and comely were they born,
Causing their mother's womb great pain;
Yet to the womb they come again.
Shiva indeed is hard to reach;
Pray, heed the doctrine this teaches you.

Lalla now considers "darling little babies" whose advent into this world causes their mothers indescribable pain. And the little pudgy ones hurt the most because of their size. Yet what lasting value does their mother's pain have? They eventually die and come right back again to cause anguish to another mother. I know how horrible this is because when I broke my legs in an accident during my second visit to India I was put into a private nursing home next door to the delivery room. Hearing those mothers crying out in panic and pain over and over–some of them calling for their mothers–was heartbreaking. My Aunt Faye more than once said to me, "Your mother went into the valley of death to bring you life." She wanted me to get the full picture of "blessed events."

78.

Itself a part of the rocky earth,
It is the self-same stone that makes
A pavement, seat or pedestal,
Or a mill-stone for a grinding mill.
Shiva indeed is hard to reach;
Then heed the doctrine this teaches you.

Our bodies are of the earth, earthly, destined to return to their original form as earth. We make many forms from life to life, but are encased in the same perishing substance. The lesson is clear: Shiva indeed is hard to reach–then heed the doctrine this teaches you.

79.

Will the sun not shine on all alike
But give heat only to holy lands?
Will Varuna not visit all homes alike
But visit only the homes of the good?
Shiva indeed is hard to reach;
Then heed the doctrine this teaches you.

Does not the sun shine with blasting heat on the both the
virtuous and the vicious equally? It is impartial. Do not virtue
and pardon of sins come to all and not the good only through the
instrument of karma? Shiva indeed is hard to reach–then heed the
doctrine this teaches you.

80.

If I knew how to control my nadis,
How to sever them from the pull of desire,
How to bind them to the inner Self,
How to cut the bonds of sorrow,
I should have known how to compound the Elixir of
    Life.
Shiva indeed is hard to reach;
Then heed the doctrine this teaches you.

Those who know how to master and direct the flow of the
life force through all the nadis–subtle energy channels–of their
bodies can sever themselves from all the controlling action of
desires and bind themselves to the inmost Self and thus cut the

bonds of sorrow, actual and potential, forever. And when that is accomplished, then create the compound of immortality. But how is it to be done? Through Soham sadhana alone. Shiva indeed is hard to reach–then heed the doctrine this teaches you.

81.

As mother a woman suckles a baby,
As wife she dallies amorously in love,
As maya she takes one's life in the end–
And yet in all these forms a woman she.
Shiva indeed is hard to reach;
Then heed the doctrine this teaches you.

Mahashakti, the feminine power inherent in all relative existence, both gives and nourishes life, only eventually to take away life. Yet she is always what she is: the creative power of life. Shiva indeed is hard to reach–then heed the doctrine this teaches you.

82.

Like a tenuous web Shiva spreads Himself,
Penetrating all frames of all things.
If while alive, you cannot see Him,
How can you see Him after death?
Think deep and sift the true Self from the self.

The Paramatman pervades all things, but its abiding time is tenuous since all things arise and dissolve perpetually. Therefore he only tenuously holds things before they are gone forever. If in this life the yogi does not find Shiva who is behind his life, how can his mind be developed enough to see Shiva when he is ejected from this world after death? Only those who can perceive and separate the true from the false Self in this very life can do so.

83.

When water freezes in the cold, it turns to snow and ice.
Reflect, O man, that one becomes three different things;
And when the sun of pure Consciousness shines,
The world of living and lifeless things, the universe and
whatever exists, are, in the Supreme, seen as one.

When Self-knowledge, Atmajnana, becomes supreme, everything is seen and known as the Self. Though there appear to be many modifications, especially the three gunas, its essence is but one. The Supreme Self, the Cosmos, and the individual Self are realized as truly The One. For the universe and those evolving within it are always one with the Source of All: Brahman. When the light of the Self shines in our consciousness, then we know this Unity to be the only truth/reality of all things, including our Self. Thus all is summed up in the single word: Shivoham–I Am Shiva. I Am That: Soham.

84.

Laughing sneezing, coughing, yawning,
Bathing in sacred pools,
Going about throughout the year,
He is about you all the time–
In all these forms recognize Him.

The first items on this list occur at random to anyone, and the sacred baths are prescribed at specific times throughout the years. But since we are surrounded at all time by God in his manifested form we must learn to perceive him.

85.

The sun sets, the moon begins to shine.
The moon sets, the mind alone is left;
The mind dissolved, nothing remains;
Bhur, Bhuvah and Swa depart.

The sun sets, the moon begins to shine. When the experience of and absorption in perception of the external objects was transcended, then heightened awareness of our internal, subjective makeup and life came into the fore.

The moon sets, the mind alone is left. When internal awareness faded away, then the mind, the organ or faculty of perception of external and internal things, remained aware of itself and functioned increasingly by intuition–direct impression without an intermediary.

The mind dissolved, nothing remains. For what remained to experience objectively, either inner or outer? Consciousness itself prevailed, of which it would not be correct to say it ever came or could possibly go. This is the eternal No Thing that is self-existent, yet whose essential existence is far beyond the "existence" of any object. Rather, it is eternal Subject. Therefore as as consequence:

Bhur, Bhuvah and Swa depart. The three worlds, material, astral and causal disappear or dissolve because they were never really there at all except as ideas arising in the principle of consciousness itself.

When Anandamayi Ma visited the Ramanashram in Tiruvana-malai, the residents there who had lived with Sri Ramana Maharshi considered her to be exactly the same as Sri Ramana and pled with her to remain with them and never leave. (When some years later in Delhi I spoke with Ma Telyarkan, one of Sri Ramana's closest devotees who was living then in Tiruvanamalai, she told me: "I found my Bhagavan in Ma.") Hearing their appeals, Ma simply said, "I neither come nor go." They understood.

86.

I burnt the foulness of my soul,
I slew my heart, its passions all,
I spread my garment's hem, and sat just there, with
    bended knees, in utter surrender unto Him.
My fame as Lalla spread afar.

Lalla burnt all the impurities of her inner and outer being, including the core of her being, and the passions and delusions that darkened them. Then she modestly spread out her clothing and sat there in meditation posture, uniting herself to the Infinite.

Then she became famous and sat there in indifference, for nothing remained to be gained or lost.

87.

The soles of my feet wore off on the roads while I wandered in search of Him.
Then lo! on a sudden, I saw that He was all and everywhere, I had nowhere to go in search of Him.
This was the Truth of a hundred truths.
Whoever learns of it, will they not wonder? Will they
   not be mad for joy?

Those who ceaselessly seek God until they can go no further, then learn that he has been with them always and everywhere. This is one of the tests of the evolving universe. It reminds me of the maxim: "Banks only loan you money if you can prove you don't need it." Only those who learn that lesson will find permanent wonder and joy.

88.

In the last watch of the moonlit night,
Remonstrating with my wayward mind,
I soothed my pain with the love of God.
Gently, gently, accosting myself,
"O Lalla, Lalla, Lalla,"
I woke my Love, my Lord and Master,
In whom absorbed, my mind was cleansed
Of its defilement by the Ten.

Evolution moves in unalterable phases. There is no Short Path except in false religion and false yoga. Certainly yogis traverse the path in differing speeds according to their diligence, but the distance is the same for all.

When she got to the last phase of the moonlight night of her mind Lalla realized that only her love, her fervent attraction for enlightenment in God, would suffice. Invoking her own Self, she awoke the deity within whose advent in her consciousness purified her inner and outer being which had been defiled by the illusions and resulting ignorance produced by her liveslong involvement in and addiction to the action of the ten indriyas (organs). They are the five organs of perception (jnanendriyas), the ear, skin, eye, tongue, and nose; and the five organs of action (karmendriyas), the voice, hand, foot, organ of excretion, and the organ of generation. Then only Spirit remained. Or had ever really been there.

89.

Let go the sacred text, the holy books,
Only the mantra sound remains.
And when the mantra sound departs,
Only the chitta is left behind.
Then lo! the chitta itself is gone,
And there is no thing left behind;
The void (shunya) merges in the Void (Shunya).

The words of the scriptures have meaning and value for us for a while, but just as babies must be weaned from the breast, so we must become free of continual involvement with them. Then only one Word remains: Soham. And when Soham is revealed/experienced as not a word or a mere sound at all, but the state of liberating enlightenment, the pure awareness of that remains until it, too, is absorbed into Primal Being. That which is beyond all word and thought and thingness merges into its infinite prototype, the Supreme Self. Then the yogi discovers that no thing is left behind, for the all-embracing No Thing is the essence of all things left behind. So he has it all, but in its reality.

Further reflection: This does not mean that scriptures will be disregarded or considered without value. Rather, the Wisdom which is the source of the scriptures will appear in the consciousness of the yogi spontaneously and he will become himself a living scripture, an embodiment of spiritual wisdom. But the mantra Soham will remain as his sadhana continues in that high state of being.

Those with an instinctive allergy to genuine sadhana and the changes it produces in the consciousness of the yogi, are enamored with the myth of "The Silence" which supposedly replaces the japa and meditation of Soham which "spontaneously drops away"–they hope. But what this really means is that the Soham mantra transforms the mind into Soham itself and is revealed as the Soham Bhava–the consciousness that is the Self and therefore liberation. No differentiation of subject-object remains. Only the Eternal Subject, the eternal Self that itself has always been Soham, will remain and not be seen as an object, but experienced as True Being: Parabrahman about which nothing can be said except that nothing can be said about It.

"The Void" is another ideal and obsession with those spiritual nihilists who cling philosophically to fundamental unconsciousness and non-existence of the Self as an ideal. But this means that the individual Self which has never been anything else but itself, and is exclusive of all that is not itself, becomes one with the Supreme Self. The dewdrop slips into the shining sea, but does not "lose" itself. It "finds" itself: the Self of its Self. As Yogananda wrote:

> I will lose myself in my Self
> In savikalpa samadhi yoga.
> I will find myself in my Self
> In nirvikalpa samadhi yoga.

There is no use trying to figure this out intellectually. We must become yogis and experience it and live it.

90.

Realization is rare indeed: seek not afar, it is near, by you.

First slay Desire, then still the mind, giving up vain imaginings;

Then meditate on the Self within, and lo! the void merges in the Void.

The first two lines are easily read or said, but how is it done? By becoming fulfilled and content in the Self and knowing that nothing else can fulfill and satisfy but the Self. For it is not love the whole world is seeking but their own reality: the Self.

Knowing the nature of the Self we seek that alone and never mistake the not-self for the Self. And though we will not despise or hate the things of the world we will know that they can never satisfy the innate attraction to the Self. So we will seek the Self above all else. "Self-controlled, cut free from desire, curbing the heart and knowing the Atman, man finds Nirvana that is in Brahman, here and hereafter"(Bhagavad Gita 5:26).

When we do not know the true nature of either our Self or the things of the world–that the Self is immortal and the entire world is perishing continually in its ever-present fluctuations and failings–we have all kinds of illusions about the world that are only fever-dreams, potentially deadly in their effect on us.

The knowledge of the Self is itself immortality and peace. That alone will satisfy us and calm our raging addictions to the ephemeral things of the world. "When he has no lust, no hatred, a man walks safely among the things of lust and hatred. To obey the Atman is his peaceful joy; sorrow melts into that clear peace: his quiet mind is soon established in peace" (Bhagavad Gita 2:64-65). "He knows peace who has forgotten desire. He lives without craving: free from ego, free from pride" (Bhagavad Gita 2:71).

"Behold, the kingdom of God is within you" (Luke 17:21), for the Self is within you. Therefore: "Only that yogi whose joy is inward, inward his peace, and his vision inward shall come to Brahman and know Nirvana" (Bhagavad Gita 5:24). For Brahman is within each one of us as the core, the center, of our Self.

We have already considered the wrong and right understanding of "void." Shunya, the No-Thing, is the Emptiness which is the only Fullness, for all things have come out from It and eventually remerge with(in) It. Our true nature is pure spirit—nothing more. And so is the Supreme Spirit in which we live eternally even now. The No-Thing is Everything and Nothing at the same time. It all depends on our viewpoint. That is why the Buddha said, "Turn around and lo! The other shore."

91.

I reined in the steed of the mind,
And, by constant practice, brought together the pranas
    coursing through the ten nadis.
Then the nectar of the Mystic Moon flowed down, suf-
    fusing my whole being,
And the void merged in the Void.

This and the next three verses are specifically about Soham Yoga.

The wild stallion of the mind must be fully controlled, otherwise there is no hope of the sadhaka attaining the final goal. He can make a great deal of progress, but eventually he will become stalled along the way, for the mind, like a horse, must be able to leap over high barriers and continue on unhindered. Sri Ramakrishna once defined a genuine sadhu as "an unsheathed sword." A genuine sadhaka is the same. By continuous practice the sadhana unites the pranas and reveals themselves as a single force. First Soham sadhana shows that all the nadis are under the rulership of the Ida and Pingala, and until these are purified and cleared of all obstruction little can be accomplished through them. Then the sadhana goes even further and perfects the functions of the Ida and Pingala, especially in relation to themselves. When this occurs, the Sushumna comes into full function—and not before, whatever the fantasies of the incompetent or badly-instructed aspirant may imagine or suppose. Then all the nadis, including the Ida and Pingala are revealed as totally under the sway of Sushumna, indeed are themselves intimately connected with the Sushumna. As the capstone, the stilled and clear mind, the consciousness, becomes merged in the Absolute Consciousness.

What I have written is just an outline. A great deal more is experienced and shown to the Soham sadhaka all along the way. I have hesitated to relate even what I have, knowing full well that the copy-cats, fantasists, fools, liars and ignoramuses will gladly seize on what I have told and claim its experience for their own—expanded by their own self-mythologies. However, I am not writing for them, but for you, the serious sadhaka and seeker for the truth about the true way of yoga: Soham Yoga.

92.

On nothing else I built my hopes,
In nothing else I put my trust—
My vakh brought me the wine I drank,
My vakh gave me the strength to seize
The darkness that within me lurked.
I rolled it up and knocked it down,
And tore it to pieces.

Lalla relied completely in her sadhana, on the Supreme Vakh, the mantra Soham, which is the original spoken form of both the

Paramatman (Brihadaranyaka Upanishad 1:4:1) and the jivatman (Brihadaranyaka Upanishad 5:15:2; Isha Upanishad, verse 16). It was Soham that brought her to the state of divine joy and Soham that empowered her to master the negative energies within her and render them easy to dispel and dissolve forever. I know this sounds very exaggerated and even irresponsible to those who have no experience of Soham sadhana. Even I was taken aback when I read the words of Sri Gajanana Maharaj and others in the Nath Yogi tradition about Soham Yoga.

For example, Gajanana Maharaj more than once cited the words of Kabir: "Rama Nama is repeated by almost all people–by thieves, by licentious people, and by rich people. But that Nama (Name) by which Dhruva and Prahlada [two children who attained spiritual perfection by calling on the Divine Name] were saved was something different." It is said that Dhruva invoked the Divine Name "Narayana," and Prahlada the Divine Name "Hari," both Names of Vishnu. Elsewhere he said the same words and added: "I boldly tell you with firm assurance that the 'different' Nama referred to by Kabir in these lines is none other than Soham. He who makes that Nama his own becomes one with the universal power. His words acquire the force of truth, and hence are full of power."

No one can be expected to believe these words outright, but I can assure you that those who begin and persevere in the japa and meditation of Soham will discover they are the simple truth. For as I explain in the second chapter of *Soham Yoga: The Yoga of the Self*, the japa of Soham becomes increasingly subtle as the yogi repeats it and undergoes a great many permutations. Thus

Soham becomes an altogether "different word" which imparts experiences and insights to the Soham yogi that he could never have dreamed were possible. I had spent half a century on various forms of yoga meditation that were only superficially different, and which all turned out to be of the same minimal character in time. So naturally I could not believe what the Nath Yogis said. But when I did what they did, I did not just believe, I perceived and knew they were telling the truth. You can do the same.

93.

Cutting my way through Six Forests,
I came upon the Digit of the Moon.
By means of the practice of prana-apana,
The world of matter shrank for me.
Then roasting my heart in the fire of love, I found my
   God.

By the means of observing the inhaling and exhaling breaths (prana and apana) continuously (prana-apana) and joining the syllable *So* to the inhalations and *Ham* to the exhalations, Lalla gained mastery of the five vital forces or pranas (see Glossary) which are the basis for all functions of the gross and subtle bodies, including the passions, the "forests" of the six evils–hunger, thirst, old age, death, grief and delusion–and passed beyond their influence forever.

Through the mastery achieved by elimination of the six evils, the "moon" of inner consciousness, which like the moon is a reflection of the "sun" of the Self, manifested and the illusions of the outer world evaporated from within her.

The seeds of karma and delusive mental states in her heart, her inmost subtle being/bodies, were roasted and could never sprout and produce more growth. In the same way, an inner consciousness (heart) that has been roasted in the fires of Soham yoga practice–tapasya–will no longer put forth shoots of the karmic seeds of earthly attachments and delusions. The world of materiality fled from Lalla as a ghost or mirage. As soon as this process of transformation was complete she entered into the full consciousness of the Self, the individual Atman which is itself the abode of the Paramatman, the Supreme Self.

94.

> When I became one with Soham,
> My body blazed as a red-hot coal,
> Then I gave up the Path of the Six,
> And betook myself to the straight true Path,
> Which led me to the Abode of Light.

When Lalla became united fully with Soham, she became one with her Self, the jivatman, and the Self of her Self, the Paramatman. Then her external being became suffused with the divine fire of purification, as a red-hot coal is suffused with material fire. Then she abandoned all attention to the entire series of Sixes:

1) The six orthodox philosophies of Hinduism: Nyaya, Vaisheshika, Sankhya, Yoga, Mimamsa, and Vedanta.

2) The six chakras: Muladhara, Swadhishthana, Manipura, Anahata, Vishuddha and Ajna

3) The six enemies to realization of the Self: desire (kama), anger (krodha), greed (lobha), arrogance (mada), delusive attachment (moha) and jealousy (matsarya).

4) The six evils of human life: hunger and thirst, old age and death, grief and delusion or loss of consciousness.

Leaving all interest in involvement with or avoidance of these elements she immersed herself in the "straight true" Path of Soham which carried her beyond all these things without her even giving them thought. For the single result of Soham sadhana–realization of the Self, the Abode of Light–completely transcended these things which then ceased to exist for her, even as possibilities.

95.

For love that would not let me be,
I, Lalla, set forth in search of Him.
And toiled and toiled for days and nights.
Then lo! the most auspicious moment of life–
I saw the Pandit in my own home.

In pondering what to say about these first two lines I vividly recalled crossing the border into Iran in 1968, when the Shah was still there. Walking into the small building to present visa and passport I saw behind the counter a man in a suit and tie, obviously educated and intelligent. When I told him I was on my way overland to India since I followed Sanatana Dharma, he looked interested and then said, "I would like to know a little bit about that religion." Being aware of how vast Dharma is, so much so that no one can encompass it all in one lifetime, I thought, "How safe it is to only want to know 'a little bit' about the Eternal Truth so there will be no danger of realizing its absolute superiority and being obligated to learn and follow it." I did not attempt to impart the desired 'little bit' to him, but smiled, got my passport stamped and continued on my way, vividly saying inwardly the words of Yogananda: "O India, I will be there!"

We must seek with deep longing to know the Self, and we must Go Forth from all that would hinder us or draw us back into the sleep of spiritual death. And we must engage in that search for many days and many nights continuously. We cannot seek in fits and starts, sometimes seeking and sometimes not seeking. Our search must be continual, encompassing day and night. The japa and meditation of Soham must be maintained perpetually. It really is a matter of life and death, spiritually speaking.

Since she persevered, "Lo! the most auspicious moment of life—I saw the Pandit (teacher of wisdom) in my own home." In the "house" of her own heart she discovered the source of wisdom: her Self.

Lalla did not just have insight into the reality of her Self, she took hold of the Self through constant Soham sadhana–and that was the "most auspicious moment of life" for her, the moment when understanding dawned and she began to walk on the way of Life Eternal.

It was no outside factor which set her feet on the path, but the internal arising of consciousness of the inner reality that was her Self.

96.

Gently, gently, I trained my mind to suspend its processes and thoughts.

Then (in the windless calm), the flame of the Lamp,
shining steady and bright, revealed my true nature
unto me.

In the dark recesses of my soul I seized upon Him and
held Him fast.

Then I diffused the inner light, (and within, without, all
was Light).

"Greater is he that is in you, than he that is in the world" (I
John 4:4) is a cardinal principle of spiritual life. The entire world
is formed of the ever-shifting energy patterns that comprise what
is known as maya–cosmic illusion. But far greater than that is the
consciousness that is the Self which is within us and is the essence
of our very existence.

False yoga deals exclusively with "energy" and "operations of
shakti." This was very prevalent in the yoga boom of the nineteen
sixties and seventies, since most of the people involved had a back-
ground in drug use. Consciousness was rarely mentioned–only
vibration and energy–for their minds were still deeply marked by
the damage and distortions resulting from drugs and "getting a
buzz." The false gurus also spoke in the same manner, since energy
(shakti) is power, and "a natural high" was the ideal and offered
result of meditation.

Therefore the practice of yoga was wrongly considered a matter
of control of inner forces, or mastery of the mind (manas/buddhi)

that was itself formed of energy. This was topped off by interest in awakening "kundalini shakti" and producing its various
phenomena. Consequently many strenuous methods were advo-
cated. I well remember an account of a supposed enlightened yogi
who described his struggle in seizing the kundalini and pulling
it upward from the base of his spine, and the way it often kept
slipping from his mental grasp and dropping back down. Just
hearing it exhausted me, but this is the way of illusion.

Lalla, however, was not deluded, but was a genuine yogini. So
instead of engaging in a wrestling match with "the serpent power"
gently she led her mind into the natural tranquility produced by
Soham sadhana.

It is really important to keep in mind when Lalla writes of any
yogic process that she was in the Nath Yogi tradition and practiced Soham sadhana: observing the natural, automatic breath and
mentally intoning *So* throughout the inhalation and *Hum* [Ham]
throughout the exhalation. When this is done while sitting with
closed eyes and awareness of the breath and the inner intonations
of Soham, that is meditation, and when it is done throughout the
rest of the yogi's waking day, that is japa (repetition).

When other types of yogic practices are engaged in, the effects
are mostly completely different in their effect and experience from
that of Soham sadhana. So when considering Lalla's Vakhs this
must be understood. What I will be writing here and later on
when needed is completely according to the practice, effects and
experiences produced by Soham Yoga.

When practicing Soham meditation, awareness of the mental
processes and external breath very early on fades away. This is

because in Soham meditation the yogi completely and naturally becomes aware of the movement of the inner breath, and since that awareness very naturally and easily replaces awareness of the physical breath, the yogi does not realize it is happening. Rather, the inner, subtle inhalation and exhalation are experienced very naturally, and in this way the yogi's mental intonations become merged in the perpetual ajapa japa of Soham–but all so easily and naturally that he may not be aware of that transfer of awareness from the outer to the inner. This is not speculation or falsehood. I experience this daily in every meditation, and so will you if you follow exactly the instructions given in *Soham Yoga* and *Light of Soham* for a sufficient amount of time.

Fake yoga and fake gurus make a big noise about "pranayama," "the breathless state," "conquering the breath," and other such things, all stemming from the fact that, however sincere they may be, the very nature of their "yoga" leads them astray and produces abnormal states in their physical and subtle bodies that are often very hard to attain–and are much worse than completely useless.

But Lalla is not a practicer of fake yoga, so she tells us that imperceptibly and completely naturally her physical breath was suspended and the inner, archetypal breath came into the foreground of her awareness. However, the yogi very likely will not be aware that his physical, lung breath has ceased, since at that time the awareness of his inner, pranic breath comes to the fore. And this is all for the best, since he might become frightened if he realizes he has "stopped breathing" in the "normal" way. At this time the calm and observant yogi will experience levels of both his mind and his breath that he never knew existed. This is the effect of his Soham sadhana, and reveals the truth of the statement made by Matsyendranath, Gorakhnath and the Yoga Chudamani Upanishad: "The inhalation comes in with the subtle sound of So, and the exhalation goes out with the subtle sound of Ham. There is no knowledge equal to this, nor has there ever been in the past or shall be in the future any knowledge equal to this. There is no japa equal to this, nor has there ever been in the past or shall be in the future any japa equal to this."

Then (in the windless calm), the flame of the Lamp, shining steady and bright, revealed my true nature unto me. This is a fact of Soham sadhana that for over fifty years of false yoga I could never have imagined to be true. Going from guru to guru and learning the "highest method known to man" from each one, I eventually saw they were all the same: momentarily interesting and certainly producing an effect–but an effect that only went so far and no farther. Actually they were almost identical in the experiences they produced. When for the sixth or seventh time I found my latest and highest practice producing exactly the same effects that all the rest had produced, I decided to just muddle through somehow and quit looking for something different–since after decades of regular practice I thought I had found that there was no something different.

But I was wrong. Soham Yoga was something different. I discovered that in the first minutes of my practice when I said to myself: "O! I love this!" And never changed my mind. The day I first began the japa and meditation of Soham was literally the happiest day of my life. I was amazed. And still am. For "the flame of the Lamp, shining steady and bright, revealed my true nature unto me."

The Soham yogi becomes inwardly aware of and observes real openings of awareness which reveal the arising of various subtle yogic kriyas (processes) about which he never knew before. And he also experiences the real kriyas about which the usual yogis only speak obliquely and without anything more than a partial understanding. He finds that all the talk he has heard or read about chakras, ida, pingala, sushumna and kundalini is just that: talk. And erroneous conclusions and mythologies without end. Suddenly there is light that dispels the fog of misinformation and error and shows the truth about these things by his own perceptions and experiences. And that insight continually increases.

In the dark recesses of my soul I seized upon Him and held Him fast. Saint Photini, the Samaritan woman in the Gospel of John, told her friends about Jesus and expressed her faith in him. Later, they came to meet Jesus and then told her, "Now we believe, not because of thy saying: for we have heard him ourselves, and know" (John 4:42). It was a result of their own experience. Without such experience "faith" usually means very little. So the wise aspirant seeks to know for himself. Otherwise he will not really know even if he believes. The yogi must never be satisfied with the assertions of others, but must always seek his own direct experience of spiritual realities. Krishna makes this clear in the Bhagavad Gita. "Since you accept me and do not question, now I shall tell you that innermost secret: knowledge of God which is nearer than knowing, open vision direct and instant. Understand this and be free for ever from birth and dying with all their evil. This is the knowledge above all other: purifier and king of secrets, only made plain to the eye of the mystic. Great is its virtue, its practice easy: thus man is brought to truth eternal" (Bhagavad Gita 9:1-2).

Then I diffused [spread forth] the inner light, and within, without, all was Light. The word translated "inner light" is *drishti*–seeing; sight; perception; insight. Light in the sense of consciousness/awareness is our inmost nature, for the Self (Atman) is itself consciousness/awareness. So *drishti* includes that. It also includes *atmabala*–soul force, the inmost power of the individual, and most of all the *atmadrishti*, the power of perception inherent in the Atman.

This inner light is an experience, but it is also a faculty, a power of the spirit. This inner light can both decrease and increase. In most people it is barely more than the glow of a firefly, but through Soham yoga sadhana it can increase and become the full enlightenment of the Self. This increase is the spreading forth of the inner light which Lalla is speaking about. No one can do it for us, nor will it happen through the passing of time. It is solely the intentional action of the yogi himself.

97.

Searching for the Self, I wearied myself;
For none by searching ever gained
The secret knowledge beyond the mind.
I stopped searching, and love led me
to the Tavern door.
There I found wine jars aplenty,
But none desiring to drink from them.

Searching for the Self, I wearied myself; for none by searching ever gained the secret knowledge beyond the mind. When we mistakenly think that the Self is an object, a thing, that can be encountered and related to in the same way we interact with material objects, we cannot possibly search in the right way, having misunderstood its fundamental nature. This is where delusive yoga comes in with its gimmicks, techniques and conditioning practices. But this "searching" never gains the Self-awareness that lies beyond the mind.

I stopped searching, and love led me to the Tavern door. There I found wine jars aplenty, but none desiring to drink from them. When the Self was no longer being related to as an external object, Lalla's intent application of will that is the true "love" led her to the inner source of spiritual bliss ("wine"). There she found ananda–joy and amrita–immortality in abundance, but no one desiring to drink of them. For only the pure Self can drink at that inmost source. "Others" cannot even draw near the depths of consciousness where immortality is found in abundance.

98.

Foulness from my mind was cleared as ashes from a mir-
ror,
Then recognition of Him came to me unmistakable and
clear.
And when I saw Him close by me,
He was all and I was not, (and there was nothing else).

Foulness from my mind was cleared as ashes from a mirror, then recognition of Him came to me unmistakable and clear. The word *mala* means taint; impurity; defilement; defect; ignorance, and limitation of consciousness. The mirrors known to Lalla were polished silver, so any dirt could be easily washed away and only the mirror itself would remain. The state of dirtiness would cease to exist. So it is with ignorance and illusion. When it is gone it is totally gone and none of its effects (defects) remain. Only the original nature of the mirror continues. This is how total and complete is the nature of enlightenment–the removal of darkness in the form of ignorance and illusion. Darkness can prevail in a cave for countless millions of years, but the moment a light is brought into it the darkness is gone! This is how drastically and permanently the state of true enlightenment is experienced.

Then recognition of Him came to me unmistakable and clear. And when I saw Him close by me, He was all and I was not, (and there was nothing else). Lalla saw the Supreme Self within her own Self and realized that It was within her as her own true being, that It was all, yet the No-Thing, and she, too, by nature was a no-thing within the No-Thing.

99.

Do away with karmas two and causes three, and you will
    be honored in the world to come.
Arise, ascend and cut through the Sun's orb, and you
    will overcome the fear of death.

Do away with karmas two and causes three, and you will be honored in the world to come. Both positive and negative karmas bind us. We should not cling to the positive and reject the negative, but go beyond them both. We must also rid ourselves of the three forms of impurity that keep us in the karmic realm of cause and effect. They are finitude in the sense of limitation, multiplicity in the sense of blindness to the unity of the individual and cosmic Selves, and the experiences of both pain and pleasure produced by reaping the results of our karma.

Arise, ascend and cut through the Suryamandala, and you will overcome the fear of death. The Suryamandala, the circle of the Sun, is the movement of the sun through the twelve signs of the zodiac, radiating the influences of both the signs themselves and the planets within those signs. Think of the sun as a magnifying glass which focuses the subtle influences upon the earth itself and all life forms living upon it—especially the human beings. All these forces are reflections of the karmic forces of the individual jivas. So to arise and cut through the Suryamandala is to depart from the body and arise to and through the sun into the higher realms of evolution. When done completely, all the karmas that would draw the individual back into rebirth in the material universe are dissolved and he goes onward into higher regions.

This is not liberation by any means, just stepping off the bottom rung of the ladder onto the rung just above it. The journey is long, but the jiva has eternity in which to accomplish it. Transcending the Suryamandala frees the jiva from fear of material rebirth, but as the jiva enters a higher realm it "dies" to the lower world and is "born" into the next higher world. And this death/birth process occurs for aeons until the jiva has transcended all "birth" through transcending all relative worlds, however subtle and advanced, and entered into Siddhaloka, the realm of the

ever-free, the nitya-siddhis. This alone is liberation in the absolute sense. Until then, even those in the highest worlds are still
samsarins. Until we pass beyond the possibility of "death" in any
form we are not free from death and truly immortal in the total
sense of the term.

100.

**Clad in the robe of jnana, on the tablet of her heart were
engraved the words that Lalla spoke,**

**And by means of the mystic syllables Soham, Lalla
merged in her chit-jyoti,**

**The luminous light of Pure Consciousness; and thus dis-
pelled the fear of death.**

The call to overcome the fear of death is not a simple message.
Lalla takes it up again in this verse. Immersing herself in jnana until
she reached Atmajnana, Lalla made the invocation of Soham her
essential consciousness until Soham Bhava became her permanent
state. For Soham alone enables the yogi to unite with the Light
of Consciousness that is the yogi's Self. Soham and the Self are
the same. Experiencing this is immortality itself in which no fear
of any kind can arise.

101.

I traversed the vastness of the Void alone, leaving behind
    me reason and sense, then came upon the secret of
    the Self;
And, all on a sudden, unexpectedly, in mud the lotus
    bloomed for me.

Jnana is not just knowledge, it is wisdom–insight, direct knowing. At the dawning of jnana the lower faculty of ordinary reason
based on sensory experience is left behind, discarded as useless.
Then alone is the secret of the Soham Self revealed. Just as the sun
arises without effort on our part, so the opening of the highest
consciousness, unforeseen by the limited mind, reveals itself in the
mud and opacity of the world and the world-bound mind. Then
there is freedom from any form of death or darkness. For death
and darkness become impossible since they are not at all real, but
only misperceptions.

102.

A tapaswin into the world came I,
And bodha illumined my path to the Self.
Alike for me is life and death:
Happy to live and happy to die,
I mourn for none, none mourns for me.

Lalla was born a yogini as a result of having traversed a long
path of evolutionary experience culminating in attaining the state
of a yoga siddha. Perfection had been attained by Lalla long before

she was born as "Lalla." The true history of every genuine yogi is the traveling of the long evolutionary path before he even becomes capable of beginning the practice of yoga–and then does so unremittingly until the goal is reached. This is hardly a hobby, an avocation: it is the very core and substance of the sadhaka's entire life. We do not just drop in for a chat with our Self occasionally, but we enter into Atmabhava permanently in time.

103.

Hoping to bloom like a cotton flower, I, Lalla, set forth in the colorful world.

But soon the cleaner and the carder came and gave me hard knocks and blows.

Spun into a gossamer yarn by a woman spinner on her spinning wheel,

I was helplessly hung upon a loom, and given more knocks from the weaver's broom.

Now turned into cloth, I was dashed and dashed by the washerman on the washing-stone.

Then into a large mortar made of stone, he threw me, and with his grimy feet, rubbed me with fuller's earth and soap.

The tailor now worked his scissors on me, and cut me with care, piece by piece.

Thus was it that I, Lalla, at last entered the High Estate of God.

The aspirant with no experience of sadhana but who has heard it praised, easily imagines himself as becoming an illumined yogi with all the powers of the universe at his command. Having read lives of great yoga siddhas, he easily sees himself as one of them. Perhaps he, too, will be written about in an inspirational book! But when the process of yoga begins to arise in him through sadhana, he finds that it is a very different matter indeed. Lalla thought she would become a little cotton flower blooming in a bright and beautiful world. But what really happened to her? The sadhana worked! And here is what it did to Lalla.

But soon the cleaner and the carder came and gave me hard knocks and blows. The cotton boll has the seed at its center. So the first step is to remove the seed by the cleaner. In modern times this is done by a cotton gin, but the process is the same as at Lalla's time: the boll is pulled apart. The carding machine which has replaced the human carder does what the human worker did: it separates the cotton fibers and pulls them straight over and over again until they are in complete alignment and do not curl in any manner. Both cleaning and carding entail the hard knocks and blows Lalla tells us about. Basically the cotton gets pulled apart and violently cleaned and straightened. But that was just the beginning. Next Lalla was...

Spun into a gossamer yarn by a woman spinner on her spinning wheel. Now Lalla was pulled out and twisted mercilessly on a spinning wheel turned by a "woman"–by her own inner energy bodies or layers of shakti. Nothing remained in its original form. Lalla did not get to drop like dew into any shining sea or merge into the void beyond all relative experience. She had a lot more to undergo.

I was helplessly hung upon a loom, and given more knocks from the weaver's broom. Those who have seen a handloom operated understand this. By means of a shuttle the thread keeps being run back and forth between the warp and woof strung on the loom, and after each passage the weaver vigorously pushes the thread into a tight compacted fabric–the steadily increasing length of cloth. But there is more coming…

Now turned into cloth, I was dashed and dashed by the washerman on the washing-stone. To both shrink the cloth into a finished form and to make it soft and wearable, it is now soaked in water and beaten violently over and over again upon a large stone in the water. So Lalla's sadhana tightened her up and literally beat her into shape by countless blows of her accumulated karmic force. The washerman of purification (shuddhi) and tapasya threw her again and again against the unyielding stone of karma resistance until the desired texture was achieved.

Then into a large mortar made of stone, he threw me, and with his grimy feet, rubbed me with fuller's earth and soap. Tossed into a confined state, by continuous yogic kriyas the "washerman" gave her a terrific drubbing with abrasive fuller's earth and soap. But that was not the end–only the beginning of a new process.

The tailor now worked his scissors on me, and cut me with care, piece by piece. Now Lalla was made to conform to a destined pattern. To do this she was cut apart and put back together with great care and precision by being pierced over and over and recombined and bound into a single unit with a needle and thread. For she was being made into something much more than raw cloth, she was being made into suitable clothing for her body that would be encased in it. In other words, she was being made a fit vessel for her jivatman to function through and attain enlightenment. All the levels her being were pulverized and pulled apart and reassembled in a completely different form or configuration than its original crude state–all through sadhana.

Thus was it that I, Lalla, at last entered the High Estate of God. Then Lalla was not at all a little cotton flower, but an abode, a robe, of God, the divine Self. God was clothed in her and she was clothed in God–a blessed interaction that culminated in the revelation of Divinity within and without.

The aspiring yogi has no idea of what will be required for him to attain siddhi and perfect Self-realization through yoga. It is just as was said about the Western Expansion movement in America: the weak died along the way and the cowards never started. But Lalla did it and so can we.

The great poet-saint Mirabai, whose devotional songs are sung throughout India, was born a princess, but was eventually expelled from the palace of her raja husband because of her refusal to abandon her spiritual life. From then on she wandered around singing her songs of love for God. In one of them she says, "I have sold everything in the marketplace of this world and bought my Khanaiya [Krishna]. Some laugh at me and say the price was too high, and some laugh and say the price was too low. But all I know is that it was all I had." Only those who give all will gain the All.

If this scares some people: Good. Yoga is not for cowards or layabouts. It is for winners, not compromisers or corner-cutters.

104.

Thou wert a royal swan once, now turned mute.
Someone, it seems, has run off with something of thine.
When the mill-stone stopped, the grain channel was
    choked with grain,
And away ran the miller with the grain.

Lalla returns to the subject of the grinding-mill mentioned in verse 28, this time as a symbol of tapasya, the purifying and refining process of yoga sadhana. She addresses the sadhaka, reminding him that in his highest nature he is a royal swan, a mystical bird that flies higher and higher into the sun, the solar world of the spirit, and transcends the bonds of the material universe and becomes freed into the boundless realm of the Spirit, the Paramatman, and thus is liberated. But although the sadhaka was once aware of this, his voice has been stilled and his awareness clouded, for his involvement with samsara has run off with this essential awareness and made him forget. In the state of forgetfulness the mill-stone of sadhana has stopped and the karmic seeds (grain) can no longer pass through it and thus be rendered of no effect. Instead they are reserved for manifestation in this or a future life. So the cycle of bondage is being perpetuated through the yogi's laxity and negligence. The solution to the problem is resumption of diligence in the practice of yoga sadhana. There is no other way.

105.

The pilgrim sannyasin goes from shrine to shrine,
Seeking to meet Him who abides within himself.
Knowing the truth, O soul, be not misled;
It is distance that makes the turf look green.

In the very ancient spiritual texts of India it is assumed that the
fourth stage of life, that of the sannyasi, is a life of perpetual wandering and the sannyasi is therefore also a yati–a wanderer. This had
two major purposes: to prevent the sadhu from becoming attached or
entrenched in any one place, and to provide access to his wisdom and
spiritual inspiration to those whom he encountered as he wandered.

This is a supremely laudable motivation, but in Lalla's time
and today sadhus wandered from holy place to holy place as a
supposedly spiritual exercise, solely for their own benefit inner
and outer. (And often just to get free food provided for them and
other pilgrims by devout people in these places. Once in India I
heard a sannyasi describe to someone at length all the best eating
spots for a monk in India.) But moving the body around while the
mind remains steady in material consciousness is a guarantee of
never finding the ever-abiding, inner Self. It only creates obsession
with where the next meal is coming from.

Knowing she could not change such pilgrims of the plate, Lalla
wisely just tells herself that is an illusion to think that a place at
a distance will provide any benefit to her inwardly or outwardly.
The spiritual grass at a distance may look greener in the wanderer's
mind, but it is a illusion. Reality–the Self–lies within.

106.

Some leave their home, some the hermitage,
But the restless mind knows no rest.
Then watch your breath, day and night,
And stay where you are.

Some people abandon their worldly life to find peace, and others abandon their monastic life for the same purpose. Both fail. For the release of the mind from all discontent occurs only through the realization of the Self. And that is done in the simplest possible way. Here is the relevant section from *Soham Yoga: The Yoga of the Self*:

Soham Yoga Sadhana In Three Sentences

The two supreme yogis of India's history, Matsyendranath and Gorakhnath, and the Yoga Chudamani Upanishad have each made three identical statements that are most important for the yogi, for they present the essence of Soham Sadhana.

1) The inhalation comes in with the subtle sound of *So*, and the exhalation goes out with the subtle sound of *Ham*.

2) There is no knowledge equal to this, nor has there ever been in the past or shall be in the future any knowledge equal to this.

3) There is no japa equal to this, nor has there ever been in the past or shall be in the future any japa equal to this.

The implication is that the unequaled, and therefore supreme, knowledge and the unequaled and supreme yoga practice are the mental intonations of *So* throughout the inhalation and *Ham* throughout the exhalation. And therefore that intoning *So* and *Ham* in time with the breath is the totality of Soham Yoga practice.

And it is *japa*: the deliberate intoning of Soham in time with the breath—not a passive listening to a sound supposed to be the ajapa japa breath sounds. (Those sounds may be heard, but only peripherally, while Soham is still being deliberately and continuously intoned inwardly in time with the breath.)

What makes the japa of Soham in time with the breath the unequaled japa? All other mantras by themselves produce a particular, intended effect. And this is of great value. But the Soham mantra does not just contain the seed-consciousness of "I Am That," the Soham Bhava. Its ajapa repetition has been going on within the yogi from eternity, before he entered into relative existence—and was then propelled along the evolutionary path by the inner power of Soham. Therefore, when repeated in time with the breath it directly joins the yogi's consciousness with his original condition, his transcendental nature. It does not just make a change in his consciousness, it moves his consciousness into its original state. Right from the start the process of Self-realization begins and moves steadily toward complete revelation of Atmabhava–Atmajnana which is the same as Brahmajnana: liberation.

Kabir has said, "If you want to know the Eternal, you will not find him in the Vedas, the shastras or in the Koran, in the temples or in the mosques. Penance, pilgrimage, breath-control, or living on nothing but neem leaves, will not lead you to him. You can find him only in your breath." (Soham: "So" when taking in and "Ham" when giving out the breath)."

107.

Should you destroy vain imaginings, desires,
which form the very web of time;
Should you realize the Lord, all-pervading
and yet untouched and pure,
You may live the life of a householder,
Or a hermit's life in a hermitage,
living the truth that you have known.

Samsara is essentially in our mind–fantasies, illusions, desires, aversions and random impulses. These are the bonds we must cast off through sadhana to transcend samsara and enter into freedom (moksha). When the ever-free Self is known within the all-embracing reality of the Paramatman, the yogi lives his external life according to his illumined will. For truth is not something we only believe, empty concepts of philosophy, but it is what we actually live. Yoga is the Life of the Self.

108.

Constantly invoking the name of Shiva,
Meditating on the Way of the Swan,
From attachment and duality set free–
Such a one, even if busily engaged
in the affairs of the world, both day and night,
Wins the favor of the God of gods.

The ultimate Name of the Shiva-Self is Soham. Soham japa and meditation are the Way of the Swan, the Self in its flight to the Absolute. Constant japa and meditation frees the Soham yogi from attachment and duality. Always inwardly flying in the Chidakasha, the Sky of Consciousness, however much the yogi may seem to be involved in the life of the world, he wins the favor of the Supreme, the Paramatman, Brahman Itself. And becomes that Supreme, the Paramatman, Brahman Itself.

109.

Some though asleep are yet awake;
Some though awake are yet asleep;
Despite ablutions some are unclean;
Despite householders' active life,
Some, by their actions, are untouched.

Some though asleep are yet awake; some though awake are yet asleep. All of us are awake deep inside even though our bodies are asleep. This world is a dream and everything in it are dream images, some of them inhabited by intelligent beings. So all are awake in the depths of their being, but most are asleep in the upper reaches of their being. Blessed are those that are awake in the dream and know it for a dream and so aspire to higher awakening.

When I was a small child I more than once dreamed that I woke up and after awhile woke up again in the dream several times. This disturbed me greatly, and I began to wonder if I would one day wake up from my continuous waking state into a completely other, higher state, and awaken even from that and keep awakening…. How could I ever know if I was ever fully awake? Actually I was seeing a hint of the truth: we can awaken into That which is beyond sleeping and waking. When I read the Bhagavad Gita I realized that I was both asleep and awake at the same time, just as a partially-sighted person is both blind and seeing simultaneously. Fortunately I discovered that yoga was the means of awakening into higher and higher levels of consciousness, passing from one dream world to another until Real Awakening into Divine Consciousness would remove sleep–and the possibility of its recurrence–forever.

Only when I found Yoga and Dharma did I understand the puzzle and begin to work it out.

Despite ablutions some are unclean. There is no doubt that since the body is mostly water it can absorb the vibrations of water which it touches. Sri Ramakrishna said, "A bath in the Ganges undoubtedly absolves one of all sins; but what does that avail? They say that the sins perch on the trees along the bank of the Ganges. No sooner does the man come back from the holy waters than the old sins jump on his shoulders from the trees. The same old sins take possession of him again. He is hardly out of the water before they fall upon him."

Why? Because his mind was not immersed in the sacred Ganges–only his body. The water never touched his mind. Others, however, who have pure minds will find that simply touching Ganges water purifies and elevates them. To drink Ganges water is a wonderful thing, but can its power reach the minds of most people? If we bathe in poison but do not swallow it, it cannot harm us. In the same way holy water, holy objects and the company of holy people do not benefit those who cannot absorb the sacred energies of those things.

Despite a householders' active life, some, by their actions, are untouched. Sri Ramakrishna said, "If you can weigh salt, you can weigh sugar," meaning that those who are competent in spiritual life are competent in worldly life, and vice-versa. Intelligence does not change when it is focused on various objects. It remains the same. So it is with inner and outer life. The Gita says, "Yoga is skill in action" (2:50), implying that it is ease and freedom from strain. The wise are free from action in the sense that it does not affect or bind them in any way. "The lotus leaf rests unwetted on water: he rests on action, untouched by action" (Bhagavad Gita 5:10).

110.

To stop a running stream, to cool a raging fire,
To roam the skies on sandaled feet,
To milk a wooden cow–
All this is fraud and jugglery.

But people under the spell of maya are attempting these things every day and fooling themselves into thinking they are succeeding. Who needs religion? Who needs its rules? Who needs yoga? They do, but they do not want to know and acknowledge that.

The running, noisy stream of their little, confined yet out of control life cannot be stopped. Day and night it flows on, yet going nowhere, really. They hold coals of burning, torturing fire that forms their tormented life and speak of how cool, how easy and how soothing it is, bringing them happiness, satisfaction and fulfillment.

They roam the sky of self-delusion and self-illusion in freedom claiming to be without a bond or a care, when all the time they are bound hand and foot and jammed into a cave of darkness and futility, even misery being a relief through distraction. The wooden dolls they consider the source and sustenance of their life are as false, barren and dry as the carved udders of a wooden cow. All this is self-fraud and self-deception on their part. "Because thou sayest, I am rich, and increased with goods, and have need of nothing; and knowest not that thou art wretched, and miserable, and poor, and blind, and naked" (Revelation 3:17).

111.

To the lake too small even for a mustard seed,
All living beings come to quench their thirst;
And into it, as soon as born, keep falling, falling,
Deer, jackal, rhinoceros, elephant seals and all.

The vast lake, the vast expanse of samsara, which seems to contain worlds beyond number and yet is seen by those with clear sight to be too small to accommodate even a single mustard seed, is sought out by sentient beings to quench their unquenchable thirst through countless lives in countless bodies, ranging from atomic gases to human forms. The moment they touch it in their minds they fall and fall and fall into it perpetually. Through creation cycles this circle of misery and futility repeats itself over and over.

112.

Three times the lake overflowed its shore;

Once its waters and the sky did meet

From Haramukh [in the north] to Kaunsar [in the south] in one vast sheet.

Seven times I saw the lake vanishing in the void (shunyankar).

I remember having seen, in former lives, through aeons of time,

These dissolutions of the worlds and their rebirth.

The overwhelming sight Lalla describes appeared to her as a miniature of the universal creation cycles which never cease. She saw the entire expanse as a single unit of water which brought to mind the Cosmic Ocean in its perpetual round of projection and withdrawal, or manifestation and dissolution. This is the way the mind of the yogi sees beyond the surface to deeper meaning at all times.

113.

However many parts I played upon the stage,

However often I quaffed that wine, the water of the Syand [river],

However many lumps of human flesh I ate,

Yet I am the same Lalla still.

What profiteth it all to me?

Through the seemingly infinite string of births in forms beyond counting or calculation–including being a fish in the Syand river and a wild animal feasting on human flesh–Lalla was at all times only a single thing: the Self. Therefore this entire panorama appeared as nothing to her. It takes a vast mind to see in vast perspective and think vast thoughts about the whole thing. Such is the perfect yogi.

114.

Throughout the ages, we have been.

Forever the sun rises and sets;

Forever Shiva creates, dissolves, and creates again.

And that's that.

115.

When the light of the day is quenched in the darkness of the night,

The earth extends to meet and dissolve in the ethereal sky,

And [on amavasya] all is blank and dark eclipse.

But strange! Raahu, the Demon of eclipse, is swallowed by the New-born Moon.

The illumination of Cit-Atman is the true worship of Shiva, the Supreme.

When the light of the Self is extinguished in the darkness and blindness of illusion everything is a single mass of blackness eclipsing the perception of all reality. But for the yogi, the eclipsing "demon" of ignorance and delusion is itself swallowed in the advent of the yogi's inner sight. Therefore Lalla says that the only true worship of the Shiva-Self is the illumination of the Self by its own flawless consciousness.

On the amavasya, the new-moon day, it is said that the demon Rahu swallows the sun. But, says Lalla, the seeker who treads the yogic path to Self-realization has the experience of the manifested universe–the sun and the sky and all the worlds–vanishing and becoming one with the unmanifested all-pervading Akshara: the imperishable, indestructible, immutable, undying, undecaying and unchanging Self that is rooted in the Supreme Self, Brahman. There, for the moment, it seems to be "dark, irretrievably dark" in the great Void; but soon it is lit up by the "new-born moon," the Parasamvit, the supreme consciousness, the supreme knowledge, which is the illumination of the higher consciousness of the Self that is itself the abode of the Supreme Shiva.

The first three lines refer to various events in which there is both end and beginning, and reversal of the "natural" samsaric order. The line that matters of the fourth one in which Lalla tells us what is the true worship of God, the true religion: illumination of the Self.

116.

They who have known the Supreme Self, Chidananda Jnanaprakasha, they are the jivanmuktas.
The ignorant add knot to knot, in hundreds, to the tangled web of samsara, its recurrent birth, its recurrent death.

They who have known the Supreme Self, Chidananda Jnanaprakasha, they are the jivanmuktas. The Self is pure consciousness (knowledge-light) alone, though it experiences millions of bodies in millions of rebirths, beginning with a single atom of hydrogen and moving upward from there to habitation in Siddhaloka itself. Though it experiences relativity, it is essentially at all times nothing but consciousness, inseparable though distinct from Brahman, the Absolute.

How can it experience all these births and all these forms it seems to inhabit, being born and dying over and over? Through the divine power we call Maya—actually, Yogamaya which *A Brief Sanskrit Glossary* defines as: "The power of Maya, of divine illusion. It is Maya in operation, the operation/movement rising from the presence (union–yoga) of God (Ishwara) within it, and therefore possessing delusive power." That is as near as anyone on this earth plane can come to a viable definition.

Yet at all times the Self is chidananda—conscious bliss. How can this be really understood or experienced? By becoming a yogi and experiencing it for ourself. It will not be an overnight attainment, but it will come to those who persevere. They, while yet alive, have gained release(from earthly births). By "alive" is meant living in a physical body, the idea being that even here in this world it is possible to become freed from further material births. This does not mean, however, that future births in astral and causal worlds will not be necessary—they will be. Simply stepping up from the first rung on the evolutionary ladder is not the end of embodiment, but only the end of material embodiment. A great deal of evolution remains, for the ladder has many rungs.

The ignorant add knot to knot, in hundreds, to the tangled web of samsara, its recurrent birth, its recurrent death. Confusion is the inescapable state of those still in earthly rebirth. It is not just a net, it is a tangled net in which we become caught over and over. Ignorant and foolish, we have added to and strengthened the net of rebirth again and again through countless lives. But freedom is possible to those who follow the advice of Sri Krishna: "Therefore be a yogi" (Bhagavad Gita 6:46).

117-118.

Who dozes off? Who is alert?

What lake constantly oozes away?

What should be offered in worship to God?

What supreme station should one gain?

It is the mind that dozes off.

It is the Akula [the Formless] that is ever alert.

The mighty senses are the lake constantly oozing out, constantly filled again.

The constant awareness of the Self is worship befitting the Lord,

And Shivahood the supreme station [state] man should gain.

It is the mind that dozes off. It is the Akula [the Formless] that is ever alert. Since it is the mind, composed of name and form, that "sleeps" and fades away, the yogi must cultivate awareness of the formless, transcendent Self that is the only reality. Involvement in the mind is sleep and awakening into the Self is just that: awakening.

The mighty senses are the lake constantly oozing out, constantly filled again. The senses are continually being depleted, which causes anxiety and even pain, but they are constantly being renewed or re-energized, so the process is repeated perpetually. This is their very nature, so they cannot be reformed or made permanent. The only solution is to go beyond them into the buddhi, the principle of Self-enlightenment. The problem cannot be resolved–only gone beyond.

The constant awareness of the Self is worship befitting the Lord. Worship of God as a separate being is false and erroneous, resulting in an abyss of confusion, conflict and error. But to live in the unbroken consciousness of Self-realization is the only true worship or religion.

And Shivahood the supreme station [state] man should gain. Not only is divinity (Shivahood) the highest state an individual should attain, it is the only state that anyone can truly attain. All else will fade away and be lost over and over until the consciousness is established in Unity.

119.

Shiva is the horse, Vishnu holds the saddle,
And Brahma the stirrups.
It is the yogi who, in the light of his yoga, knows
Which god can mount the horse.

Shiva is the horse, Vishnu holds the saddle, and Brahma the stir-rups. There is only one Supreme Being, but that Being is so vast and beyond our powers of conception that in order to speak of It–especially in relation to human beings–a tremendous amount of symbolism must be used. Here Lalla is referring to the Trimurti–Brahma, Vishnu and Shiva–who represent the divine processes of creation, maintenance, and dissolution (not destruction, for dissolution is liberation–deliverance) within relative existence.

It is the yogi who, in the light of his yoga, knows which god can mount the horse. The yogi, through the insight his practice of Soham yoga has produced in him, can perceive which process (which god) is guiding his life as a horseman controls and directs a horse. And he should either change or confirm it. If Brahma is directing him, he will be oriented toward control and alteration of his external, material life. If Vishnu is directing him, he will be oriented toward the harmonious integration, maintenance and stabilization of his material and mental life together. If Shiva the Great Yogi is directing him, he will be oriented toward the spiritualization of his entire life in all its aspects by the practice of Soham yoga sadhana, purifying evolving all the aspects of his inner and outer being with the ultimate goal of transmuting them into the pure consciousness that is his Self, and thereby becoming fully liberated from all that is not the Self and transcending all lesser modes of being and literally and permanently to Abide In The Self As The Self.

But how is that accomplished? Lalla continues:

120.

He who is the eternal Anahata,

The ever-unobstructed sound of Soham;

Whose is the all-permeating form of the etherial sky;

Whose dwelling is the vast transcendent Void;

Who has no name, caste, gotra, nor form;

Who is Pure, Undifferentiated Self-awareness;

Who is "Nada-Bindu," the Logos and the Light–

He is the God Who mounts the horse.

Brahman Itself is Soham, the eternal, unprojected and therefore self-existent Sound. It is Itself the Chidakasha, the infinite Space (Ether) of Consciousness. Yet It is simultaneously the Infinite Dweller of the Chidakasha. The sound of Soham is eternally arising in the depths of Brahman–and therefore in the depths of every sentient being. It has no name–designation in the sense of a descriptive word–because its origin is beyond name. It is nameless because Brahman is Nameless, and it is one with Brahman and IS Brahman. It has no conditioning attributes such as name, caste, gotra (family lineage) or form, and it has no genealogy in the sense of having come into existence or manifestation from something other than Itself. It has no "history," for it is not in time even now. It is Eternity itself in this world of time and space and change. It has no form because it has no modifications nor is it "inside" something. It transcends and is untouched by time, space and all conditionings.

It is itself the Self-existent. Yet at the same time it is all things by its nature as both Sound and Consciousness which manifests as individuality in all things and is therefore absolute Unity. This is why the Brihadaranyaka Upanishad (1:4:1) tells us: "In the beginning this (world of relative manifestation/existence) was only the Supreme Self [Paramatman], in the shape of a person [Parampurusha]. Looking around he saw nothing else than the Self. He first said, 'I am Soham' [Soham asmi]". So the awareness "I exist" or "I am" is itself Soham—not just its relative manifestation.

Soham alone "mounts the horse" as the ruler-director, of the yogi which in time is revealed to the yogi as both his own Self (Jivatman) and the Supreme Self (Paramatman), the very root of his own existence. Therefore, the yogi, too, says: Soham Asmi. It is the totality of his being.

121.

Would you understand what Oneness is?
It has turned me into nothingness.
Though He is One, Alone, and All,
Yet I am caught in the War of Two.
Though He has neither color nor form,
Yet I am caught in His wondrous forms.

This is perhaps the most intriguing verse of Lalla. She tells us that understanding Oneness turns you into nothingness: no-thing-ness. This is actually logical, since only Brahman is absolutely One, and those who unite with Brahman transcend all relative existence where "things" or even qualities can exist. Touching the One transforms us into the No Thing Itself. Yet as long as we remain in the sphere of relative existence we are caught in duality, and although what we see is really only the One which is beyond attributes or form, yet we are entranced by the infinite glories and forms of the Absolute–even if in essence It does transcend them!

In the Bhagavad Gita (11:10-13) Arjuna is shown the universal form(s) of God: "Speaking from innumerable mouths, seeing with a myriad eyes, of many marvelous aspects, adorned with countless divine ornaments, brandishing all kinds of heavenly weapons, wearing celestial garlands and the raiment of paradise, anointed with perfumes of heavenly fragrance, full of revelations, resplendent, boundless, of ubiquitous regard. Suppose a thousand suns should rise together into the sky: such is the glory of the Shape of Infinite God. Then the son of Pandu beheld the entire universe, in all its multitudinous diversity, lodged as one being within the body of the God of gods." He is naturally overwhelmed by this vision. And so is Lalla. But she is not speechless! In most of the remaining verses she will eloquently convey her experience.

122.

He is in myriad colors and forms. Seek Him out.
Patiently suffer whatever your lot, and happy be.
Anger and hate and enmity, you must destroy.
All this done, though hard it be: Behold your God.

This is extremely clear. There is no need to analyze it, but we must get busy and follow it. How? Through yoga! We need to tell ourselves this a lot and follow our own advice.

123.

I roamed the ten directions and pierced the wind and the void.

I closed the nine gates of the body and shut out the Thirty-six.

Wherever I looked, I found the Lord, within, without, and in the Void.

The purpose of yoga is the purification, clarification, expansion, development and evolution of the mind. That means the mind has to travel meaningfully in a lot of directions. Yoga is for adults who can understand and control their minds and the directions it goes in. No human being on earth is as unique and complex as an adept yogi. Intelligence and right judgment are essentials, as well. And yoga opens it all up to the yogi.

It takes audacity and courage to be a yogi, and enormous power of will. The will and courage it took for Magellan to sail around the world for the first time in its history, and thus to prove that the earth is round, is necessary for success in yoga. The yogi is a wonder in the world. And I hope from this that you can draw two conclusions: 1) There are hardly any real yogis in the world. 2) For you to be a yogi you must become more than human. You must become a god. And you will not have much company on the path to the Infinite. In fact, you may be the only one walking it. And if you cannot, will not or do not want to forge ahead and make it on your own... then you won't.

But Lalla did. She mastered all the directions the mind can travel, she went beyond the wind and kicked aside "the void" of

No Thing. She sealed the nine chakras—the nine entries of cosmic energy into her physical, astral and causal bodies—in perfect union and passed utterly beyond the thirty-six cosmic principles of which relative existence consists from top to bottom. (For information and analysis regarding the nine chakras, see Chapter Four, The Yogi's Subtle Anatomy, in *Soham Yoga: The Yoga of the Self*).

Then and only then did she even look for the Supreme, and found It within, without and in the Nowhere which is really the Everywhere.

And she did this with just one thing: SOHAM.

124.

I turned to Him heart and soul,
And heard the ringing of the Bell of Truth.
There, in dharana, fixed in thought,
I soared the Sky and the Region of Light.

Lalla's turning to Him in totality was Soham.

The Bell of Truth which she both rang and heard as herself was Soham.

The Dharana in which her consciousness became fixed was Soham.

The Universal Chidakasha, the Infinite Light in which she rose, was Soham.

125.

I searched within for the Mystic Moon,
For like seeks out the like.
Thou art all this and this and this;
There is none else but Thee.
What then is the meaning of Thy sport,
Of Thy creation's wondrous forms?

Lalla searched solely within for that jivatman which reflected the light of the Paramatman, for only like can seek out like and find the Like. She clearly saw that Brahman was all that can be designated or perceived as "this and this and this"–there is only The One. And she asks: What is the meaning of the One manifesting in many forms? But she gives no answer....

126.

O Lord of the Dark Blue Throat,
I have the very same Six Thou hast.
And yet, estranged from Thee,
I suffer misery.
There surely is this difference:
Thou art the master of the Six,
But by the Six I have been robbed.

O Lord of the Dark Blue Throat. Shiva is said to have a blue throat (nilkantha–though in this verse the word Lalla uses is shyamagala) from drinking poison at the beginning of creation so it would not harm anyone.

I have the very same Six Thou hast. There are six attributes of Divine Being: Sovereign Power (Maya Shakti), Omnipotence (Sarvakar-tritva), Omniscience (Sarvajnatva), All-inclusiveness (Purnatva), Eternality (Nityatva) and All-pervasiveness (Vyapakatva). Being made in the divine image and likeness, humans have the same attributes in a finite manner, whereas in God they are infinite.

And yet, estranged from Thee, I suffer misery. Since we exist solely in the Paramatman, Brahman, if we fall into forgetfulness–and therefore alienation to that reality–we cannot help but fall also into the various miseries of relative existence which produce in us a multitude of pain-bearing illusions and delusions. Alienated from our own ultimate Self, this is a spiritual death that produces a state worse than any mere physical death.

There surely is this difference: Thou art the master of the Six, but by the Six I have been robbed. As a bent lens or mirror will distort that which is reflected or perceived, so the human being, though possessing the divine attributes in himself, will misperceive, misapply and misuse them to his own harm and virtual self-annihilation. Instead of realities the six become tormenting hallucinations like the fever dreams resulting from severe or mortal illness. In the grip of false perceptions the human being can only live irrationally and perpetually harm himself. This is truly the condition of a living hell.

127.

Lord, I did not know who I was,
nor Thou, the Supreme Lord of all.
I knew only this body of mine always.
The relation between Thou and me,
That Thou art I and I am Thou and both are one, I did
    not know.
[But now I know], To ask: "Who art Thou,
who am I?" is doubt of doubts.

Lord, I did not know who I was, nor Thou, the Supreme Lord of all. Until we experience our true nature as spirit which is in truth a part of Brahman, we do not at all know either Brahman or ourselves. We are like someone who sees himself in a mirror for the first time and asks, "Who is that?"

I knew only this body of mine always. This is because we identify with the body and say such things as "I am sick" or "I am dying" when it is the body alone that is sick or dying. And naturally we become attached to the body and call it "me" and value it above all else, thinking that without it we would not exist–not knowing that within the body is the true "I" the true Self.

The relation between Thou and me–that Thou art I and I am Thou and both are one–I did not know. And not knowing the truth of ourselves, the state of irrevocable union with Brahman, we identify and become involved and obsessed with the untruth that we think is us. Consequently we do not know that we and Brahman are one–though not the same, since Brahman is infinite and we are finite. We both are the same as Brahman and are different from

Brahman. But the difference is not separation, only distinction of ourselves from Brahman. This is totally impossible to understand, but it can be experienced and known by the yogi who frees and transmutes his consciousness by Soham yoga sadhana.

[But now I know], to ask: *"Who art Thou, who am I?" is doubt of doubts.* Once we know who/what we really are and Who/What Brahman is, then we have no more doubt and misunderstanding. We know it by directly being and experiencing fully what we and Brahman are. Tennyson wrote of this mystic puzzle:

> Flower in the crannied wall,
> I pluck you out of the crannies,
> I hold you here, root and all, in my hand,
> Little flower—but if I could understand
> What you are, root and all, all in all,
> I should know what God and man is.

Notice that he says, "what God and man *is*," not "*are*."

Sri Ramakrishna said that when there is a banquet there is conversation, but when all have eaten they leave in silence. In the same way, once the yogi has become "full" in his experience of the Self, there is no more talk, only satisfaction.

128.

I, Lalla, entered by the garden-gate of mine own mind,
And there, O joy! saw Shiva with Shakti sealed in one;
And there itself I merged in the Lake of Immortal Bliss.
Now while alive I am unchained from the wheel of birth
    and death,
What can the world do unto me?

I, Lalla, entered by the garden-gate of mine own mind. This is an
extremely important statement, for the Self is entered only through
the gate of the mind. The mind itself is dual. It is both the manas,
the sensory mind, and the buddhi, the intelligence–the intellect. In
meditation the yogi joins these two in a union in which at first they
reflect one another and then they absorb-assimilate one another.

And there, O joy! saw Shiva with Shakti sealed in one. Thus the
union of Shiva and Shakti takes place on the level of the individual
and on the level of the universal. Lalla realized her Self as Shiva
and Shakti merged on these two levels.

And there itself I merged in the Lake of Immortal Bliss. In this
manner she was merged in the perception of That Which Itself is
Immortal Bliss (Ananda).

*Now while alive I am unchained from the wheel of birth and
death. What can the world do unto me?* Although in the body,
Lalla has become liberated from the cycle of birth and death. And
therefore truly is no longer in the world, which as a consequence
cannot even touch her in any manner or even be in any relation
to her. She is truly a siddha-purusha, transcending all duality and
dwelling totally in the state of Unity. This is absolute Fearlessness.

129.

Thou dost pervade all shapes and forms,
Thou breathest life into all frames,
The whole creation hums with Thy silent sound.
Who can measure the Immeasurable, O Lord!

Lalla in this manner addresses Brahman as Soham, the silent sound which pervades the entire range of existence, immanent and transcendent. Nothing can encompass the unencompassable essence that is Soham.

130.

He who regards himself and others alike,
He who regards alike both day and night,
He whose mind is free from duality–
He alone has seen the God of gods.

There is real non-dualism (advaita) and also false non-dualism. The real thing is a genuine seeing and experiencing of unity. Just parroting "it is all one" is meaningless and is ultimately detrimental. If we actually see unity we will not have to keep saying it like a recording. Such a habit is usually a way to evade realistic evaluation and to deny the practical and obvious. Also, duality is not some ghost to shoo away with a positive platitude. Either we see unity or we do not. Pretense is never wisdom.

Both duality and unity are real. Duality is necessary for us to even function realistically. When you become hungry you eat. That is duality. You are not one with the food, otherwise you would not be hungry. When someone asks you for aid, it would be both insulting and idiotic to say, "It is all one" and go your way. I once read about a group of militant cultists who said to someone who objected to their non-dual bullying: "Look man, you're making duality!" What foolishness–and evil. As long as we are in the realm of duality, things are dual. However, the is wisdom in realizing that all things come from The One and all things share a common existence in The One. But for our evolution we have come into relative existence–or into the experience of relative existence–in order to evolve into direct experience of the Unity, not just to have faith in it and become a nuisance to both ourselves and others. Regarding this Sri Ramakrishna said the following.

"Let me tell you a story. In a forest there lived a holy man who had many disciples. One day he taught them to see God in all beings and, knowing this, to bow low before them all.

"A disciple went to the forest to gather wood for the sacrificial fire. Suddenly he heard an outcry: 'Get out of the way! A mad elephant is coming!' All but the disciple of the holy man took to their heels. He reasoned that the elephant was also God in another form. Then why should he run away from it? He stood still, bowed before the animal, and began to sing its praises. The mahut of the elephant was shouting: 'Run away! Run away!' But the disciple didn't move. The animal seized him with its trunk, cast him to one side, and went on its way. Hurt and bruised, the disciple lay unconscious on the ground. Hearing what had happened, his teacher and his brother disciples came to him and carried him to the hermitage. With the help of some medicine he soon regained consciousness.

"Someone asked him, 'You knew the elephant was coming–why didn't you leave the place?' 'But', he said, 'our teacher has told us that God Himself has taken all these forms, of animals as well as men. Therefore, thinking it was only the elephant God that was coming, I didn't run away.'

"At this the teacher said: 'Yes, my child, it is true that the elephant God was coming; but the mahut God forbade you to stay there. Since all are manifestations of God, why didn't you trust the mahut's words? You should have heeded the words of the mahut God.'

"It is said in the scriptures that water is a form of God. But some water is fit to be used for worship, some water for washing the face, and some only for washing plates or dirty linen. This last sort cannot be used for drinking or for a holy purpose. In like manner, God undoubtedly dwells in the hearts of all–holy and unholy, righteous and unrighteous; but a man should not have dealings with the unholy, the wicked, the impure. He must not be intimate with them. With some of them he may exchange words, but with others he shouldn't go even that far. He should keep aloof from such people."

This is just good sense. If the supposed non-dualists really believe in unity, why are they so hostile, rude and bullying to those who are "making duality?" It reminds me of an incident in the first year or so that I was a yogi.

A fellow yogi whom I had admired and respected began drifting away from the yoga life. The first symptom was his reading and citing books of false non-dualism. And having become a "jnani" he became increasingly rude and contemptuous of everyone else.

One evening I was sitting in a small vegetarian restaurant when someone asked me my opinion of one of the non-dual teacher-gods Jack worshipped. I said that I would not give my opinion, but that I would tell him the history of this "non-dualist" and he could form his own opinion. After I had said just a few sentences, Jack interrupted, almost shouting: "Just tell me this! Is everything Divine Mother, or not?" This amused me, because this advaita deity I was speaking of mocked the concept of "Divine Mother" which Jack was evoking. So I answered, "Yes. Everything is Divine Mother, so will you please shut up, Divine Mother, and let Divine Mother as me continue giving an answer to a question I was asked–and not you?" Grumbling, he sat there and shuffled, breathing hard in exasperation, and soon left. A short time after this he moved away to an isolated place hundreds of miles distant. A yogi friend of mine who had been a close friend of Jack's for several years went all the way there to see him. She found him appallingly ravaged from alcohol and drugs. Jack immediately told her that he did not want to hear any "yogi or devotee talk," because the only thing that interested him any more was sex. (He did not express it as genteelly as I have.) And that concluded the career of Non-dual Jack. Well, he did say he was intent on just one thing, so that is a form of non-duality isn't it?

131.

By oft-repeated practice, the wide expanse of the manifested universe is lifted to absorption;
And the saguna world, of forms and qualities, merges
  in the vastness of the Void with a splash of water on
  water falling;
Then the ethereal Void dissolves, and the Ineffable Supreme alone remains.
This, O Bhatta [Brahmin Pandit], is the Truth to gain.

First it must be kept in mind that every human being is a
miniature universe. My friend, Dr. Judith Tyberg, who was a great
Sanskrit scholar, told me that when she was doing advanced study
at Benares Hindu University a lecturer came who displayed a map
of the universe and the chart of *Gray's Anatomy* depicting the
human body. He showed the many correspondences between the
two, demonstrating that the human body is a living model of the
universe. In actuality, the individual Self descends into material
incarnation in the very same stages that the cosmos is projected
into objective existence. And the process of the withdrawal (pralaya) of the universe and the individual jiva follow the same order
or pattern. This is because the microcosm is a reflection of the
macrocosm. Soham Yoga accomplishes this consciously through
the will and practice (abhyasa) of the individual yogi. Nothing
is haphazard, but occurs in precise order just as the cosmos is
projected and withdrawn in exact order. So that is what is being
described here as the experience of the adept sadhaka.

By oft-repeated practice, the wide expanse of the manifested universe is lifted to absorption. Reading this I remembered hearing, when I was nine or ten years old, a man telling of his spiritual awakening. He said: "At first I thought, 'The whole world has changed.' But then I realized that that world had not changed at all: *I had changed.* And my 'new me' naturally saw it in an all new manner."

Therefore Lalla is not just speaking of an observed experience, but of a state of consciousness that is also a state of being. So this is not some kind of philosophical insight but a thorough transformation of perception by means of a thoroughly transformed mind. And this occurs only "by repeated practice" of yoga: Soham sadhana. It is a matter of resolution (laya) of the yogi's consciousness into its higher levels. In Soham meditation it is possible for the yogi to experience the ascent of his awareness to the levels in his subtle bodies that correspond to the higher stages of consciousness from which he descended to external, material awareness. It is this yogic process Jesus was meaning when he said: "Arise, let us go hence" (John 14:31).

It is not the external universe that has been withdrawn into its Source, but externalized consciousness has been elevated and returned to its original state of Self-awareness. "The Ineffable Supreme alone remains." And this is the true doctrine of authentic yoga: Soham sadhana.

The individual is a miniature universe, containing within himself all the levels of existence physical, astral and causal. Originally he was a point of consciousness within the Infinite Consciousness, but extended himself through a series of expansions to encompass the three level of manifestation–physical, astral and causal.

Through Soham yoga the consciousness of this diversity is transformed into consciousness of/and is perfect Unity. That is what this Vakh is all about: a purely subjective experience/practice in which the focus of the mind rises to increasingly subtler levels of the individual's manifested being, which in time results in a permanent state of awareness of the jivatman, the individual spirit, within the Paramatman, the Supreme Spirit which is the basis of all existence.

This alone is yoga: Soham Asmi–I Am Soham (Brihadaranyaka Upanishad 1:4:1, 5.15.2. Isha Upanishad 16.) Soham Asmi–"I am That I am"–is exactly what God told Moses was his Name in Exodus 3:14.

And the saguna world, of forms and qualities, merges in the vastness of the Void with a splash of water on water falling. The entire range of relative existence from highest to lowest is saguna and therefore is experienced by those whose consciousness is oriented toward the conditioned and the changeable. The transcendent realm of existence/consciousness, the Chidakasha, is beyond such relative perceptions because only the consciousness of Oneness (Advaita) prevails there. *A Brief Sanskrit Glossary* defines it: "The Space (Ether) of Consciousness. The infinite, all-pervading expanse of Consciousness from which all 'things' proceed; the subtle space of Consciousness in the Sahasrara (Thousand-petalled Lotus). The true 'heart' of all things. Brahman in Its aspect as limitless knowledge; unbounded intelligence. This is a familiar concept of the Upanishads. It is not meant that the physical ether is consciousness.

The Pure Consciousness (Cit) is like the ether (Akasha), an all-pervading continuum."

*Then the ethereal Void dissolves, and the Ineffable Supreme alone
remains.* All that is relative in the yogi becomes resolved or returned
to its original state of being that is Pure Consciousness. In one
sense we can call it a transmutation, but it reality it is not an actual
change but a recovery of what the yogi has always been. It is both
Return and Revelation.

This, O Bhatta [Brahmin Pandit], is the Truth to gain. The only
true upadesha, spiritual teaching, is the Realization of the Self–not
just words of philosophy or ideas about the Self.

132.

Here there is neither word nor thought,
Transcendent nor non-Transcendent here.
Vows of silence and mystic mudras
cannot gain you admittance here.
Even Shiva and Shakti remain not here.
The Somewhat that remains is the Truth
to know and realize.

Here there is neither word nor thought. Not only "is neither word
nor thought" proceeding from the mind, the manas, the manas
itself is not there. This implies two things: 1) the mind cannot
reach that state of enlightenment; and 2) the mind no longer exists
in that state of enlightenment. It is important to realize that the
manas is absent in that state, but Lalla does not say the buddhi,
the intellect/intelligence is not there, for it is. Thought is the

province of the manas, but direct knowledge through intuition is the province of the buddhi. This state is known as buddhi-sattwa, the experience of the buddhi in its most subtle level in which the buddhi and the Self are virtually indistinguishable. It is also the experience of I-am (asmita/aham)–experience of the Self through the buddhi. And this is perfectly encapsulated in the declaration: Soham Asmi–I Am Soham.

Transcendent nor non-Transcendent here. When we get beyond space there is no Up or Down. In the same way when we have entered into the Self there is nothing to either transcend or not transcend. An entirely other State of Being prevails. Sri Ramakrishna put it this way: "Once a salt doll went to measure the depth of the ocean. It wanted to tell others how deep the water was. But this it could never do, for no sooner did it get into the water than it melted. Now who was there to report the ocean's depth? Then the 'I', which may be likened to the salt doll, melts in the Ocean of Existence-Knowledge-Bliss Absolute [Satchidananda] and becomes one with It. Not the slightest trace of distinction is left. Reaching the seventh plane, the mind is annihilated; man goes into samadhi. What he feels then cannot be described in words."

Vows of silence and mystic mudras cannot gain you admittance here. Nothing relative or finite can lead to the Infinite Absolute.

Even Shiva and Shakti remain not here. The duality of Consciousness and Energy disappears and becomes non-existent in that state, for there is only the One which is both and at the same time neither of them, for their perception depends upon an observer and the power of observation, both of which are relative in character and therefore no longer there. Instead there is Unified Consciousness.

The Somewhat that remains is the Truth to know and realize. It is not Nothing, but rather is the No-Thing. We cannot even accurately say it exists, for it is Existence Itself, Total Being in which no kind of duality exists even as an illusion or misperception. It cannot really be explained or described because language is formulated on sensory and subject/object experience which in that state is left behind. And what "remains" is what the liberated siddhas teach but never really speak or describe. Only a yogi can make sense of this.

133.

Here there is neither you and I,
No "postulated thought," nothing to contemplate,
Even the All-Creator is forgotten.
The ignorant blind cannot see the Ineffable Supreme hard to know.
But the pure, the wise, having seen merge in the Supreme.

In THAT there is nothing but Thatness—Absolute Unity. So there is no you/I axis on which to base dualistic consciousness—for dualism is *un*consciousness, not consciousness. There is no object to perceive, much less contemplate and draw conclusions about. When all creation has been transcended, where can be even the thought or concept of an All-Creator? Pure Being alone remains, and is all that ever has been.

Ajnanatimira, the glaucoma of ignorance, blinds all to the presence of the Ineffable Supreme which is hard to know, since there is no thing that can perceive or understand Its existence–especially since it does not "exist" the way relative, limited things do. External existence is really non-existence, a mirage. But those who purify themselves in the fires of yoga sadhana see the Absolute, and instantly, simultaneously, experience It as their own true being. For them Seeing is Becoming. The salt doll merges into the Ocean.

134.

Thou wert absorbed in Thine Own Self, hidden from
   me.
I passed whole days in seeking Thee out.
But when I saw Thee in mine own Self, O joy!
Then Thou and I disported ourselves in ecstasy.

Thou wert absorbed in Thine Own Self, hidden from me. The Nath Yogis have a very important principle: All the seeking is on the part of the seeker, not the sought. This is a reflection of the way things are for the authentic sadhaka. God is not "seeking" or "calling" or "drawing" the "devotee" as in the ideas of the "bhakti" tradition. Rather the sadhaka on his own has to become awake to the existence of the Absolute and then to seek It on his own initiative and through the application of his own will. Considering that the Absolute is his own Self, he could do nothing other than exactly that.

I passed whole days in seeking Thee out. Lalla spent not just many days of a single life, she spent entire lifetimes in seeking the One Reality.

But when I saw Thee in mine own Self, O joy! Then Thou and I disported ourselves in ecstasy. Becoming a yogi, Lalla then searched within, and in finding her true Self found the Infinite Self, the Paramatman. Like two mirrors reflecting one another they continually flowed into one another and yet were only One. Each was the Self of the other, not an object. Again: only the yogi understands this.

136.

The chitta, the mind, is ever new,

The ever-changing moon is new,

And ever new the shoreless expanse of waters that I have
    seen.

Since I, Lalla, have scoured my body and mind, (emp-
    tied it of dead yesterdays and tomorrows unborn),

I live in the ever-present Now, (and all things always are
    to me) forever new and new.

The chitta, the mind, is ever new, the ever-changing moon is new, and ever new the shoreless expanse of waters that I have seen. There is a configuration of energy that is considered the mind. But it is really only an instrument of the mind which in essence is consciousness (chit). The substance of the mind is chitta, the subtle energy that is the substance of the mind, and therefore the true mind itself. It is the field of the mind, the field of consciousness, and consciousness itself which includes the subconscious mind.

Because of its subtle, rarified nature, the chitta is ever-new in the sense that time and change cannot touch it, nor can the higher reaches of the yogi's perception, "the ever-changing moon," be touched by time and change. This is because they both are really extensions or reflections of the shoreless expanse of Consciousness that is the Ultimate Reality in which the chitta and the higher mind exist and are are illumined.

Since I, Lalla, have scoured my body and mind, (emptied it of dead yesterdays and tomorrows unborn), I live in the ever-present Now, (and all things always are to me) forever new and new. Having rid herself of the karmas, samskaras and vasanas formed in her past that could manifest as an equally confined and conditioned future, Lalla lived in the timeless, unconditioned Now of her own liberated Self. This eternal Now, having no past or future duality, is therefore "forever new and new" in the sense of every moment being the eternal Now. No past. No future. Just Being.

137.

Whatever work I did became worship of the Lord;
Whatever word I uttered became a mantra;
Whatever this body of mine experienced became
The sadhanas of Shaiva Marga illumining my path to
    Paramashiva.

Having become permanently established in the Eternal Consciousness that is Shiva, everything Lalla did became a manifestation, an extension or action of Shiva (the Shiva Tattwa or

Principle). Everything became simultaneously Path and Goal, Yoga Sadhana and Liberation. Their essence was revealed as The One.

And thus the sadhana of Lalla was completed. And so is this commentary.

Did you enjoy reading this book?

Thank you for taking the time to read *The Inspired Wisdom of Lalla Yogeshwari*. If you enjoyed it, please consider telling your friends or posting a short review at Amazon.com, Goodreads, or the site of your choice.

Word of mouth is an author's best friend and much appreciated

GET YOUR FREE
MEDITATION GUIDE

Sign up for the Light of the Spirit Newsletter and get
Learn How to Meditate Effectively.

Get free updates: newsletters, blog posts, and podcasts, plus
exclusive content from Light of the Spirit Monastery.

Visit: https://ocoy.org/newsletter-registration

GLOSSARY

Abhyasa: Sustained (constant) spiritual practice.

Ajapa Japa: A yogic term that means the natural, spontaneous sound of the breath that goes on perpetually through the simple act of breathing. This sound is extremely subtle, and though non-verbal is the highest form of mantra. The Mantra "So'ham" (I am That) which is produced by the breath itself, without any conscious effort at repeating it: the inhalation sounding 'So' and the exhalation 'ham.'

Ajapa Gayatri: So'ham Mantra.

Ajnana: Ignorance; nescience.

Ajnanatimira: The glaucoma of ignorance

Ajnani: One who is ignorant, devoid of knowledge and wisdom.

Akasha: Ether; space; sky; literally: "not visible." The subtlest of the five elements (panchabhuta), from which the other four arise. It is all-pervading, and is sometimes identified with consciousness–chidakasha. It is the basis of sound (shabda), which is its particular property.

Akshara: Imperishable; indestructible, immutable, undying; undecaying; unchanging–all in reference to the individual self and the Supreme Self, Brahman.

Akula: Without form; formless.

Amavasya: New moon day.

Amrita: That which makes one immortal. The nectar of immortality that emerged from the ocean of milk when the gods churned it.

Anahata: "Unstruck;" "unbeaten." Continuous bell-like inner resonance; the heart; the heart chakra; the inner divine melody (mystic sounds heard by the Yogis); supernatural sound; So'ham.

Ananda: Bliss; happiness; joy. A fundamental attribute of Brahman, which is Satchidananda: Existence, Consciousness, Bliss.

Anandamaya kosha: "The sheath of bliss (ananda)." The causal body (karana sharira). The borderline of the Self (atman).

Anandamayi Ma: One of the major spiritual figures in twentieth-century India, first made known to the West by Paramhansa Yogananda in his Autobiography of a Yogi.

Annamaya kosha: "The sheath of food (anna)." The physical–or gross–body, made of food.

Arya(n): One who is an Arya–literally, "one who strives upward." Both Arya and Aryan are exclusively psychological terms having nothing whatsoever to do with birth, race, or nationality. In his teachings Buddha habitually referred to spiritually qualified people as "the Aryas." Although in English translations we find the expressions: "The Four Noble Truths," and "The Noble Eightfold Path," Buddha actually said: "The Four Aryan Truths," and "The Eightfold Aryan Path."

Atmabala: Soul-force.

Atmabhava: The nature of the Self; awareness of the self; feeling: "I am the Self."

Atmabodha: Knowledge of the Self; also a work of that name by Sri Sankara.

Atmadarshan: The seeing or sight of the Self (atma); the vision of the Self; knowledge of the Self through direct vision or knowing; the vision of seeing everything as the Self.

Atmadrishti: Atma-darshan.

Atma(n): The individual spirit or Self that is one with Brahman; the essential being, nature or identity of each sentient being.

Atmajnana: Direct knowledge of the Self; Brahma-Jnana.

Atmajnani: One who has atmajnana.

Bhava: Subjective state of being (existence); attitude of mind; mental attitude or feeling; state of realization in the heart or mind.

Bindu: Point; dot; seed; source; the creative potency of anything where all energies are focused.

Brahmajnana: Direct, transcendental knowledge of Brahman; Self-realization.

Brahmajnani: One who possess Brahmajnana.

Brahman: The Absolute Reality; the Truth proclaimed in the Upanishads; the Supreme Reality that is one and indivisible, infinite, and eternal; all-pervading, changeless Existence; Existence-knowledge-bliss Absolute (Satchidananda); Absolute Consciousness; it is not only all-powerful but all-power itself; not only all-knowing and blissful but all-knowledge and all-bliss itself.

Brahmana: A knower of Brahman; a Brahmajnani.

Brahmin (Brahmana): A knower of Brahman; a member of the highest Hindu caste traditionally consisting of priests, pandits, philosophers, and religious leaders.

Buddhi: Intellect; intelligence; understanding; reason; the thinking mind; the higher mind, which is the seat of wisdom; the discriminating faculty.

Buddhi-sattwa: Experience of the buddhi in its most subtle level in which the buddhi and the Self are virtually indistinguishable; the experience of I-am (asmita/aham), experience of the Self through the buddhi.

Caste: (Literally: color.) In traditional Hindu society there were four divisions or castes according to the individual's nature and aptitude: Brahmin, Kshatriya, Vaishya, and Shudra.

Chidakasha: "The Space (Ether) of Consciousness." The infinite, all-pervading expanse of Consciousness from which all "things" proceed; the subtle space of Consciousness in the Sahasrara (Thousand-petalled Lotus). The true "heart" of all things. Brahman in Its aspect as limitless knowledge; unbounded intelligence. This is a familiar concept of the Upanishads. It is not meant that the physical ether is consciousness. The Pure Consciousness (Chit) is like the ether (Akasha), an all-pervading continuum.

Chit: Consciousness (that is spirit or purusha); "to perceive, observe, think, be aware, know;" pure unitary Consciousness. The principle of universal intelligence or consciousness.

Chitta: The subtle energy that is the substance of the mind, and therefore the mind itself; mind in all its aspects; the field of the mind; the field of consciousness; consciousness itself; the subconscious mind.

Chit-jyoti: The Light of Consciousness; the Illumination that is the Self.

Daityas: Demons who constantly war with the gods. Sometimes "races" or nationalities who acted contrary to dharma and fought against the "aryas" were also called demons (daityas or asuras); giant; titan.

Dharana: Concentration of mind; fixing the mind upon a single thing or point. "Dharana is the confining [fixing] of the mind within a point or area" (Yoga Sutras 3:1).

Dharma: The righteous way of living, as enjoined by the sacred scriptures and the spiritually illumined; law; lawfulness; virtue; righteousness; norm.

Dhruva: A child who performed intense tapasya to attain the vision of Vishnu; permanent; fixed; steady.

Dhyana(m)/Dhyana Yoga: Meditation; contemplation.

Drishti: Seeing; sight; vision; view; opinion; gaze; perception.

Dwandwa(s): The pairs of opposites inherent in nature (prakriti) such as pleasure and pain, hot and cold, light and darkness, gain and loss, victory and defeat, love and hatred.

Dwesha: Aversion/avoidance for something, implying a dislike for it. This can be emotional (instinctual) or intellectual. It may range from simple non-preference to intense repulsion, antipathy and even hatred. See Raga.

Gajanana Maharaj: Sri Gajanana Maharaj (Gajanan Murlidhar Gupte) of Nasik in western India (Maharashtra state) was a saint of the Nath Sampradaya in the first half of the twentieth century.

Gorakhnath/Gorakshanath: A master yogi of the Nath Yogi (Nath Pantha) tradition. His dates are not positively known, but he seems to have lived for many centuries and travelled throughout all of India, Bhutan, Tibet, and Ladakh teaching philosophy and yoga.

Gotra: Clan; family; lineage.

Guna: Quality, attribute, or characteristic arising from nature (Prakriti) itself; a mode of energy behavior. As a rule, when "guna" is used it is in reference to the three qualities of Prakriti, the three modes of energy behavior that are the basic qualities of nature, and which determine the inherent characteristics of all created things. They are: 1) sattwa–purity, light, harmony; 2) rajas–activity, passion; and 3) tamas–dullness, inertia, and ignorance.

Gunatita: Beyond the Gunas; one who has transcended the three Gunas.

Indriya: Organ. The five organs of perception (jnanendriyas) are the ear, skin, eye, tongue, and nose. The five organs of action (karmendriyas) are the voice, hand, foot, organ of excretion, and the organ of generation.

Ishwarapranidhana: Offering of one's life to God.

Jiva: Individual spirit.

Jivatma(n): Individual spirit; individual consciousness.

Jnana(m): Knowledge; knowledge of Reality–of Brahman, the Absolute; also denotes the process of reasoning by which the Ultimate Truth is attained. The word is generally used to denote the knowledge by which one is aware of one's identity with Brahman.

Jnanamaya kosha: "The sheath of intellect (buddhi)." The level of intelligent thought and conceptualization. Sometimes called the Vijnanamaya kosha. The astral-causal body.

Jnanendriyas: The five organs of perception: ear, skin, eye, tongue, and nose.

Jnani: A follower of the path of knowledge (jnana); one who has realized–who knows–the Truth (Brahman).

Kabir: An Indian mystic of the fifteenth and sixteenth centuries.

Kama: Desire; passion; lust.

Kamandalu: A water vessel carried by a traveling sannyasi; usually made of a gourd or coconut shell, it may also be earthenware. The kamandalu and staff (danda) are considered the insignia of the sannyasi along with gerua clothing.

Karma: Karma, derived from the Sanskrit root kri, which means to act, do, or make, means any kind of action, including thought and feeling. It also means the effects of action. Karma is both action and reaction, the metaphysical equivalent of the principle: "For every action there is an equal and opposite reaction." "Whatsoever a man soweth, that shall he also reap" (Galatians 6:7). It is karma operating through the law of cause and effect that binds the jiva or the individual soul to the wheel of birth and death. There are three forms of karma: sanchita, agami, and prarabdha. Sanchita karma is the vast store of accumulated actions done in the past, the fruits of which have not yet been reaped. Agami karma is the action that will be done by the individual in the future. Prarabdha karma is the action that has begun to fructify, the fruit of which is being reaped in this life.

Karmendriyas: The five organs of action: voice, hand, foot, organ of excretion, and the organ of generation.

Karmic: Having to do with karma.

Kosha: Sheath; bag; scabbard; a sheath enclosing the soul; body. There are five such concentric sheaths or bodies: the sheaths of bliss, intellect, mind, life-force and the physical body–the anandamaya, jnanamaya, manomaya, pranamaya and annamaya bodies respectively.

Krodha: Anger, wrath; fury.

Kula: Possessing a form.

Kumar(a): A male virgin.

Kumaras (Four): At the beginning of this creation cycle the four most advanced human souls (Sanaka, Sanandana, Sanatkumara and Sanatsujata) from the previous cycle refused to engage in the creation of the world and to enter into worldly life despite the command of Brahma that they do so. Instead they engaged in intense yoga and attained liberation. The chief of these was Sanatkumara who thereby became the Lord of Liberation for all humanity. Ever present in subtle form, Sanatkumara assists those who truly seek liberation–usually invisibly and unknown to them. But at their attainment of perfect realization he reveals himself to them and leads them to the worlds beyond compulsory rebirth.

Kundalini: The primordial cosmic conscious/energy located in the individual; it is usually thought of as lying coiled up like a serpent at the base of the spine.

Kusha: One of the varieties of sacred grass (darbha) used in many religious rites. Because of its insulating qualities, both physical and metaphysical, it is recommended as a seat (asana) for meditation, and as mats for sleeping (it keeps the sleeper warm).

Lalla Yogeshwari: A great fourteenth century Kashmiri yogini and mystic, the first poet in the Kashmiri language, whose mystic verses called Vakhs are popular even today.

Laya: Dissolution; merging.

Lobha: Greed; covetousness.

Mahabhutas: The Five Elements (Panchabhuta): ether (akasha), air (vayu), fire (agni), water(ap), and earth (prithvi).

Mahapralaya: The final cosmic dissolution; the dissolution of all the worlds of relativity (Bhuloka, Bhuvaloka, Swaloka, Mahaloka, Janaloka, Tapaloka, and Satyaloka), until nothing but the Absolute remains. There are lesser dissolutions, known simply as pralayas, when only the first five worlds (lokas) are dissolved.

Mala: Taint; impurity; defilement; defect; ignorance, limitation of consciousness.

Manana: Thinking, pondering, reflecting, considering.

Manas(a): The sensory mind; the perceiving faculty that receives the messages of the senses.

Mandala: Region; sphere or plane, e.g., Suryamandala or the solar region; a yantra-design made on a metal plate or drawn with auspicious elements upon which ritualistic worship is performed.

Manomaya kosha: "The sheath of the mind (manas–mental substance)." The level (kosha) of the sensory mind. The astral body.

Mantra(m): Sacred syllable or word or set of words through the repetition and reflection of which one attains perfection or realization of the Self. Literally, "a transforming thought" (manat trayate). A mantra, then is a sound formula that transforms the consciousness.

Mantra Yoga: The Yoga of the Divine Word; the science of sound; the path to divine union through repetition of a mantra—a sound formula that transforms the consciousness.

Mantra chaitanya: The dormant potency of a Mantra.

Mantra shakti: Power of the Lord's Name; the potency of any Mantra.

Mantra siddhi: Perfection in the practice of Mantra-Japa; mastery over the Devata of a Mantra so that the Devata graces the votary whenever invoked.

Mantric: Having to do with mantra(s)—their sound or their power.

Matsyendranath: Guru of Gorakhnath and the first publicly known Nath Yogi, having become a disciple of Adinath who is considered an avatar of Shiva. As with Gorakhnath, we have no dates for him.

Maya: The illusive power of Brahman; the veiling and the projecting power of the universe, the power of Cosmic Illusion. "The Measurer"—a reference to the two delusive "measures," Time and Space.

Mayic: Having to do with Maya.

Moksha: Release; liberation; the term is particularly applied to the liberation from the bondage of karma and the wheel of birth and death; Absolute Experience.

Mukta: One who is liberated–freed–usually in the sense of one who has attained moksha or spiritual liberation.

Mukta purusha: A person liberated from all kinds of bondage; One freed from birth and death.

Mukti: Moksha; liberation.

Nada: Sound; the resonance of sound; mystic inner sound; the primal sound or first vibration from which all creation has emanated; the first manifestation of the unmanifested Absolute; the inner sound of a mantra experienced in meditation.

Nama: Name. The Divine Name.

Nath Yogi: A member of the Nath Yogi Sampradaya.

Nath Yogi Sampradaya: An ancient order of yogis claiming Matsyendranath, Gorakhnath, Patanjali, Jnaneshwar and Jesus (Isha Nath) among their master teachers.

Nirguna: Without attributes or qualities (gunas).

Nirvikalpa: Indeterminate; non-conceptual; without the modifications of the mind; beyond all duality.

Nirvikalpa Samadhi: Samadhi in which there is no objective experience or experience of "qualities" whatsoever, and in which the triad of knower, knowledge and known does not exist; purely subjective experience of the formless and qualitiless and unconditioned Absolute. The highest state of samadhi, beyond all thought, attribute, and description.

Nitya: Eternal; permanent; unchanging; the ultimate Reality; the eternal Absolute.

Pandit(a): Scholar; pundit; learned individual; a man of wisdom.

Paramahan[m]sa/Paramhan[m]sa: Literally: Supreme Swan, a person of the highest spiritual realization, from the fact that a swan can separate milk from water and is therefore an apt symbol for one who has discarded the unreal for the Real, the darkness for the Light, and mortality for the Immortal, having separated himself fully from all that is not God and joined himself totally to the Divine, becoming a veritable embodiment of Divinity manifested in humanity.

Paramatma(n): The Supreme Self, God.

Paramhansa: See Paramahan[m]sa/Paramhan[m]sa above.

Param[a]samvit: Supreme consciousness; supreme knowledge.

Prahlada: A daitya prince who rejected his daitya heritage and became a devotee of Vishnu. His father, the evil Hiranya-kashipu, tortured him and attempted his life because of his devotion and his speaking to others of divine matters, yet he remained steadfast.

Prakriti: Causal matter; the fundamental power (shakti) of God from which the entire cosmos is formed; the root base of all elements; undifferentiated matter; the material cause of the world. Also known as Pradhana. Prakriti can also mean the entire range of vibratory existence (energy).

Prakritilaya: Absorbed or submerged in Prakriti; the state of yogis who have so identified with the cosmic energy that they are trapped in it as though in a net and cannot separate them-selves from it and evolve onwards until the cosmic dissolution (pralaya) occurs in which the lower worlds of men, angels, and archangels (bhur, bhuwah and swar lokas) are dissolved.

Pralaya: Dissolution. See Mahapralaya.

Prana: Life; vital energy; life-breath; life-force; inhalation. In the human body the prana is divided into five forms: 1) Prana, the prana that moves upward; 2) Apana: The prana that moves downward, producing the excretory functions in general. 3) Vyana: The prana that holds prana and apana together and produces circulation in the body. 4) Samana: The prana that carries the grosser material of food to the apana and brings the subtler material to each limb; the general force of digestion. 5) Udana: The prana which brings up or carries down what has been drunk or eaten; the general force of assimilation.

Pranamaya kosha: "The sheath of vital air (prana)." The sheath consisting of vital forces and the (psychic) nervous system, including the karmendriyas.

Puja: Worship; ceremonial (ritual) worship; adoration; honor. Usually involving the image of a deity.

Pujari: One who performs ritualistic worship (puja).

Raga: Blind love; attraction; attachment that binds the soul to the universe. Attachment/affinity for something, implying a desire for it. This can be emotional (instinctual) or intellectual. It may range from simple liking or preference to intense desire and attraction. Greed; passion. See Dwesha.

Ram/Rama: An incarnation of God–the king of ancient Ayodhya in north-central India. His life is recorded in the ancient epic Ramayana.

Rama Nama: The name of Rama–both of the Absolute Brahman and of the incarnation, Rama of Ayodhya–used in devotional singing, japa and meditation.

Ramakrishna, Sri: Sri Ramakrishna lived in India in the second half of the nineteenth century, and is regarded by all India as a perfectly enlightened person–and by many as an Incarnation of God.

Sadhaka: One who practices spiritual discipline–sadhana–particularly meditation.

Sadhana: Spiritual practice.

Sadhana Shakti: Both the power to successfully engage in sadhana, the the power that accrues within the sadhaka from his practice of sadhana.

Sadhu: Seeker for truth (sat); a person who is practicing spiritual disciplines; a good or virtuous or honest man, a holy man, saint, sage, seer. Usually this term is applied only to monastics.

Sadhvi: A female "sadhu."

Saguna: Possessing attributes or qualities (gunas).

Samadhi: The state of superconsciousness where Absoluteness is experienced attended with all-knowledge and joy; Oneness; here the mind becomes identified with the object of meditation; the meditator and the meditated, thinker and thought become one in perfect absorption of the mind.

Samsara: Life through repeated births and deaths; the wheel of birth and death; the process of earthly life.

Samsara chakra: The wheel of birth and death.

Samsari: The transmigrating soul.

Samsaric: Having to do with samsara; involved with samsara; partaking of the traits or qualities of samsara.

Samsarin: One who is subject to samsara–repeated births and deaths–and who is deluded by its appearances, immersed in ignorance.

Samskara: Impression in the mind, either conscious or subconscious, produced by action or experience in this or previous lives; propensities of the mental residue of impressions; subliminal activators; prenatal tendency. See Vasana.

Samshaya: Doubt; suspicion.

Sanatana Dharma: "The Eternal Religion," also known as "Arya Dharma," "the religion of those who strive upward [Aryas]." Hinduism.

Sanatana Dharmi: One who both believes in and follows the principles of Sanatana Dharma.

Sanatkumaras: The Four Kumaras (see Kumaras).

Sannyas(a): Renunciation; monastic life. Sannyasa literally means "total throwing away," in the sense of absolute rejection of worldly life, ways and attitudes. True sannyas is based on viveka and vairagya. It is not just a mode of external life, but a profound insight and indifference to the things of the world and the world itself–not the world of God's creation, but the world of human ignorance, illusion, folly and suffering which binds all sentient beings to the wheel of continual birth and death. The sannyasi's one goal is liberation through total purification and enlightenment. His creed is Shankara's renowned Vedanta in Half a Verse: "Brahman is real. The world is illusion. The jiva is none other than Brahman."

Sannyasi(n): A renunciate; a monk.

Sannyasic: Pertaining to sannyasa and the life and thought of a sannyansin.

Sannyasini: A female renunciate; a nun.

Sanskrit: The language of the ancient sages of India and therefore of the Indian scriptures and yoga treatises.

Santosha: Contentment; joy; happiness; peacefulness.

Satchidananda: Existence-Knowledge-Bliss Absolute; Brahman.

Sattwa: Light; purity; harmony, goodness, reality.

Sattwa Guna: Quality of light, purity, harmony, and goodness.

Savikalpa: With doubt and change.

Savikalpa Samadhi: Samadhi in which there is objective experience or experience of "qualities" and with the triad of knower, knowledge and known; lesser samadhi; cognitive samadhi; samadhi of wisdom; meditation with limited external awareness. Samprajñata samadhi.

Shaiva/Shaivite: A worshipper of Shiva; pertaining to Shiva.

Shakti: Power; energy; force; the Divine Power of becoming; the apparent dynamic aspect of Eternal Being; the Absolute Power or Cosmic Energy; the Divine Feminine.

Shaucha: Purity, cleanliness

Shiva: A name of God meaning "One Who is all Bliss and the giver of happiness to all." Although classically applied to the Absolute Brahman, Shiva can also refer to God (Ishwara) in His aspect of Dissolver and Liberator (often mistakenly thought of as "destroyer").

Shuddha: Pure; clear; clean; untainted.

Shuddha-chaitanya: Pure intelligence; pure consciousness.

Shuddhi: The state of purity (shuddha); purification.

Shunya: Void; no-thing; emptiness.

Siddha: A perfected–liberated–being, an adept, a seer, a perfect yogi.

Siddha Nama: The Perfect Name; a title of the Soham Mantra.

Siddha Purusha: A perfectly enlightened being.

Siddhaloka: The highest realm of existence in which the fully liberated (siddhas) live. (However, wherever a siddha is, that place is siddhaloka.)

Siddhi: Spiritual perfection; psychic power; power; modes of success; attainment; accomplishment; achievement; mastery; supernatural power attained through mantra, meditation, or other yogic practices. From the verb root sidh–to attain.

Soham: "That am I;" the ultimate Atma mantra, the mantra of the Self; the Ajapa Gayatri formula of meditation in which "So" is intoned mentally during natural inhalation and "Ham" is intoned mentally during natural exhalation. Soham is pronounced "Sohum," as the short "a" in Sanskrit is pronounced like the American "u" in "up."

Soham Bhava: The state of being and awareness: "THAT I am." Gorakhnath says that So'ham Bhava includes total Self-comprehension (ahamta), total Self-mastery (akhanda aishwarya), unbroken awareness of the unity of the Self (swatmata), awareness of the unity of the Self with all phenomenal existence–as the Self (vishwanubhava), knowledge of all within and without the Self–united in the Self (sarvajñatwa).

Surya: The sun; the presiding deity of the sun, sometimes identified with Vishnu (Surya-Narayana) or the Absolute Brahman.

Surya-mandala: The circle (orbit) of the sun.

Swadhyaya: Introspective self-study or self-analysis leading to self-understanding. Study of spiritual texts regarding the Self.

Tamas: Dullness, darkness, inertia, folly, and ignorance.

Tamasic: Possessed of the qualities of the tamo guna (tamas). Ignorant; dull; inert; and dark.

Tantra: A manual of, or a particular path of, sadhana laying great stress upon japa of a mantra and other esoteric practices relating to the powers latent in the human complex of physical, astral, and causal bodies in relation to the cosmic Power usually thought as the Divine Feminine.

Tantrika: Pertaining to Tantra.

Tapas: See tapasya.

Tapasya: Austerity; practical (i.e., result-producing) spiritual discipline; spiritual force. Literally it means the generation of heat or energy, but is always used in a symbolic manner, referring to spiritual practice and its effect, especially the roasting of karmic seeds, the burning up of karma.

Tapaswi(n): Ascetic; one who is practising Tapas.

Tattwa: "Thatness." Principle; element; the essence of things; truth; reality.

Tilak: A sacred mark made on the forehead or between the eyebrows, often denoting what form of God the person worships.

Upadesha: Spiritual instruction; the instructions given by the guru at the time of initiation; initiation itself.

Urmi: A wave; an evil; reference is often made to six evils; they are hunger and thirst, old age and death, grief and delusion or loss of consciousness.

Vairagya: Non-attachment; detachment; dispassion; absence of desire; disinterest; or indifference. Indifference towards and disgust for all worldly things and enjoyments.

Vaishnava: A devotee of Vishnu.

Vaishnavism: A religious sect of Hinduism, whose members follow the path of devotion to God as Vishnu or one of Vishnu's avatars–especially Sri Rama, Sri Krishna, and (in Bengal) Sri Chaitanya.

Vak: Speech.

Vakh: Vak; Speech.

Vakya: That which is denoted by speech.

Varuna: A Vedic deity considered the sustainer of the universe and also the presiding deity of the oceans and water. Often identified with the conscience.

Vasana: Subtle desire; a tendency created in a person by the doing of an action or by experience; it induces the person to repeat the action or to seek a repetition of the experience; the subtle impression in the mind capable of developing itself into action; it is the cause of birth and experience in general; an aggregate or bundle of samskaras–the impressions of actions that remain unconsciously in the mind.

Vasana(s): A bundle or aggregate of such samskaras.

Viveka: Discrimination between the Real and the unreal, between the Self and the non-Self, between the permanent and the impermanent; right intuitive discrimination.

Vrata: Vow; a resolution; rule of conduct; a vow of abstinence.

Yama: Yamaraja; the Lord of Death, controller of who dies and what happens to them after death.

Yantra: Geometrical designs of the energy patterns made by mantras when they are recited or which, when concentrated on produce the effects of the corresponding mantras. Though often attributed to deities, they are really the diagrams of the energy movements of those deities' mantras.

Yati: Wanderer; a wandering ascetic.

Yoga: Literally, "joining" or "union" from the Sanskrit root yuj. Union with the Supreme Being, or any practice that makes for such union. Meditation that unites the individual spirit with God, the Supreme Spirit. The name of the philosophy expounded by the sage Patanjali, teaching the process of union of the individual with the Universal Soul.

Yoga Siddha: One who is perfected in yoga and therefore totally liberated and united with Brahman.

Yogamaya: The power of Maya, of divine illusion. It is Maya in operation, the operation/movement rising from the presence (union–yoga) of God (Ishwara) within it, and therefore possessing delusive power.

Yogananda (Paramhansa): The most influential yogi of the twentieth century in the West, author of Autobiography of a Yogi and founder of Self-Realization Fellowship in America.

Yogi: One who practices Yoga; one who strives earnestly for union with God; an aspirant going through any course of spiritual discipline.

Yogic: Having to do with Yoga.

Yogini: A female practicer of yoga.

ABOUT THE AUTHOR

Swami Nirmalananda Giri (Abbot George Burke) is the founder and director of the Light of the Spirit Monastery (Atma Jyoti Ashram) in Cedar Crest, New Mexico, USA.

In his many pilgrimages to India, he had the opportunity of meeting some of India's greatest spiritual figures, including Swami Sivananda of Rishikesh and Anandamayi Ma. During his first trip to India he was made a member of the ancient Swami Order by Swami Vidyananda Giri, a direct disciple of Paramhansa Yogananda, who had himself been given sannyas by the Shankaracharya of Puri, Jagadguru Bharati Krishna Tirtha.

In the United States he also encountered various Christian saints, including Saint John Maximovich of San Francisco and Saint Philaret Voznesensky of New York. He was ordained in the Liberal Catholic Church (International) to the priesthood on January 25, 1974, and consecrated a bishop on August 23, 1975.

For many years Swami Nirmalananda has researched the identity of Jesus Christ and his teachings with India and Sanatana Dharma, including Yoga. It is his conclusion that Jesus lived in India for most of his life, and was a yogi and Sanatana Dharma missionary to the West. After his resurrection he returned to India and lived the rest of his life in the Himalayas.

He has written extensively on these and other topics, many of which are posted at OCOY.org.

Atma Jyoti Ashram
(Light of the Spirit Monastery)

Atma **Jyoti Ashram** (Light of the Spirit Monastery) is a monastic community for those men who seek direct experience of the Spirit through yoga meditation, traditional yogic discipline, Sanatana Dharma and the life of the sannyasi in the tradition of the Order of Shankara. Our lineage is in the Giri branch of the Order.

The public outreach of the monastery is through its website, OCOY.org (Original Christianity and Original Yoga). There you will find many articles on Original Christianity and Original Yoga, including *The Christ of India*. *Foundations of Yoga* and *How to Be a Yogi* are practical guides for anyone seriously interested in living the Yoga Life.

You will also discover many other articles on leading an effective spiritual life, including *Soham Yoga: The Yoga of the Self* and *Spiritual Benefits of a Vegetarian Diet*, as well as the "Dharma for Awakening" series—in-depth commentaries on these spiritual classics: the Bhagavad Gita, the Upanishads, the Dhammapada, the Tao Teh King and more.

You can listen to podcasts by Swami Nirmalananda on meditation, the Yoga Life, and remarkable spiritual people he has met in India and elsewhere, at http://ocoy.org/podcasts/

READING FOR AWAKENING

Light of the Spirit Press presents books on spiritual wisdom and Original Christianity and Original Yoga. From our "Dharma for Awakening" series (practical commentaries on the world's scriptures) to books on how to meditate and live a successful spiritual life, you will find books that are informative, helpful, and even entertaining.

Light of the Spirit Press is the publishing house of Light of the Spirit Monastery (Atma Jyoti Ashram) in Cedar Crest, New Mexico, USA. Our books feature the writings of the founder and director of the monastery, Swami Nirmalananda Giri (Abbot George Burke) which are also found on the monastery's website, OCOY.org.

We invite you to explore our publications in the following pages.

Find out more about our publications at
lightofthespiritpress.com

BOOKS ON MEDITATION

Soham Yoga
The Yoga of the Self
A complete and in-depth guide to effective meditation and the life that supports it, this important book explains with clarity and insight what real yoga is, and why and how to practice Soham Yoga meditation.

Discovered centuries ago by the Nath yogis, this simple and classic approach to self-realization has no "secrets," requires no "initiation," and is easily accessible to the serious modern yogi.

Includes helpful, practical advice on leading an effective spiritual life and many Illuminating quotes on Soham from Indian scriptures and great yogis.

"This book is a complete spiritual path." –Arnold Van Wie

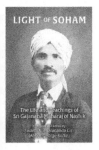

Light of Soham
The Life and Teachings of Sri Gajanana Maharaj of Nashik
Gajanan Murlidhar Gupte, later known as Gajanana Maharaj, led an unassuming life, to all appearances a normal unmarried man of contemporary society. Crediting his personal transformation to the practice of the Soham mantra, he freely shared this practice with a small number of disciples, whom he simply called his friends. Strictly avoiding the trap of gurudom, he insisted that his friends be self-reliant and not be dependent on him for their spiritual progress. Yet he was uniquely able to assist them in their inner development.

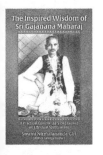

The Inspired Wisdom of Gajanana Maharaj
A Practical Commentary on Leading an Effectual Spiritual Life
Presents the teachings and sayings of the great twentieth-century Soham yogi Gajanana Maharaj, with a commentary by Swami Nirmalananda.

The author writes: "In reading about Gajanana Maharaj I encountered a holy personality that eclipsed all others for me. In his words I found a unique wisdom that altered my perspective on what yoga, yogis, and gurus should be.

"But I realized that through no fault of their own, many Western readers need a clarification and expansion of Maharaj's meaning to get the right understanding of his words. This commentary is meant to help my friends who, like me have found his words 'a light in the darkness.'"

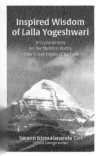

Inspired Wisdom of Lalla Yogeshwari
A Commentary on the Mystical Poetry of the Great Yogini of Kashmir
Lalla Yogeshwari was a great fourteenth-century yogini and wandering ascetic of Kashmir, whose mystic poetry were the earliest compositions in the Kashmiri language. She was in the tradition of the Nath Yogi Sampradaya whose meditation practice is that of Soham Sadhana: the joining of the mental repetition of Soham Mantra with the natural breath.

Swami Nirmalananda's commentary mines the treasures of Lalleshwari's mystic poems and presents his reflections in an easily intelligible fashion for those wishing to put these priceless teachings on the path of yogic self-transformation into practice.

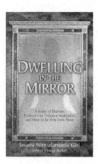

Dwelling in the Mirror
A Study of Illusions Produced By Delusive Meditation And How to Be Free from Them

Swami Nirmalananda says of this book:

"Over and over people have mistaken trivial and pathological conditions for enlightenment, written books, given seminars and gained a devoted following.

"Most of these unfortunate people were completely unreachable with reason. Yet there are those who can have an experience and realize that it really cannot be real, but a vagary of their mind. Some may not understand that on their own, but can be shown by others the truth about it. For them and those that may one day be in danger of meditation-produced delusions I have written this brief study."

BOOKS ON YOGA & SPIRITUAL LIFE

Satsang with the Abbot
Questions and Answers about Life, Spiritual Liberty, and the Pursuit of Ultimate Happiness

The questions in this book range from the most sublime to the most practical. "How can I attain samadhi?" "I am married with children. How can I lead a spiritual life?" "What is Self-realization?" "How important is belief in karma and reincarnation?"

In Swami Nirmalananda's replies to these questions the reader will discover common sense, helpful information, and a guiding light for their journey through and beyond the forest of cliches, contradictions, and confusion of yoga, Hinduism, Christianity, and metaphysical thought.

Foundations of Yoga
Ten Important Principles Every Meditator Should Know

An introduction to the important foundation principles of Patanjali's Yoga: Yama and Niyama

Yama and Niyama are often called the Ten Commandments of Yoga, but they have nothing to do with the ideas of sin and virtue or good and evil as dictated by some cosmic potentate. Rather they are determined by a thoroughly practical, pragmatic basis: that which strengthens and facilitates our yoga practice should be observed and that which weakens or hinders it should be avoided.

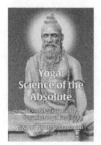

Yoga: Science of the Absolute
A Commentary on the Yoga Sutras of Patanjali

The Yoga Sutras of Patanjali is the most authoritative text on Yoga as a practice. It is also known as the Yoga Darshana because it is the fundamental text of Yoga as a philosophy.

In this commentary, Swami Nirmalananda draws on the age-long tradition regarding this essential text, including the commentaries of Vyasa and Shankara, the most highly regarded writers on Indian philosophy and practice, as well as I. K. Taimni and other authoritative commentators, and adds his own ideas based on half a century of study and practice. Serious students of yoga will find this an essential addition to their spiritual studies.

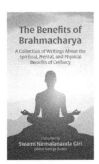

The Benefits of Brahmacharya
A Collection of Writings About the Spiritual, Mental, and Physical Benefits of Continence

"Brahmacharya is the basis for morality. It is the basis for eternal life. It is a spring flower that exhales immortality from its petals." Swami Sivananda

This collection of articles from a variety of authorities including Mahatma Gandhi, Sri Ramakrishna, Swami Vivekananda, Swamis Sivananda and Chidananda of the Divine Life Society, Swami Nirmalananda, and medical experts, presents many facets of brahmacharya and will prove of immense value to all who wish to grow spiritually.

Living the Yoga Life
Perspectives on Yoga

"Dive deep; otherwise you cannot get the gems at the bottom of the ocean. You cannot pick up the gems if you only float on the surface." Sri Ramakrishna

In *Living the Yoga Life* Swami Nirmalananda shares the gems he has found from a lifetime of "diving deep." This collection of reflections and short essays addresses the key concepts of yoga philosophy that are so easy to take for granted. Never content with the accepted cliches about yoga sadhana, the yoga life, the place of a guru, the nature of Brahman and our unity with It, Swami Nirmalananda's insights on these and other facets of the yoga life will inspire, provoke, enlighten, and even entertain.

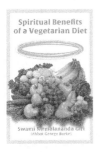

Spiritual Benefits of a Vegetarian Diet

The health benefits of a vegetarian diet are well known, as are the ethical aspects. But the spiritual advantages should be studied by anyone involved in meditation, yoga, or any type of spiritual practice.

Diet is a crucial aspect of emotional, intellectual, and spiritual development as well. For diet and consciousness are interrelated, and purity of diet is an effective aid to purity and clarity of consciousness.

The major thing to keep in mind when considering the subject of vegetarianism is its relevancy in relation to our explorations of consciousness. We need only ask: Does it facilitate my spiritual growth–the development and expansion of my consciousness? The answer is Yes.

BOOKS ON THE SACRED SCRIPTURES OF INDIA

The Bhagavad Gita for Awakening
A Practical Commentary for Leading a Successful Spiritual Life

Drawing from the teachings of Sri Ramakrishna, Jesus, Paramhansa Yogananda, Ramana Maharshi, Swami Vivekananda, Swami Sivanana of Rishikesh, Papa Ramdas, and other spiritual masters and teachers, as well as his own experiences, Swami Nirmalananda illustrates the teachings of the Gita with stories which make the teachings of Krishna in the Gita vibrant and living.

From *Publisher's Weekly*: "[The author] enthusiastically explores the story as a means for knowing oneself, the cosmos, and one's calling within it. His plainspoken insights often distill complex lessons with simplicity and sagacity. Those with a deep interest in the Gita will find much wisdom here."

The Upanishads for Awakening
A Practical Commentary on India's Classical Scriptures

The sacred scriptures of India are vast. Yet they are only different ways of seeing the same thing, the One Thing which makes them both valid and ultimately harmonious. That unifying subject is Brahman: God the Absolute, beyond and besides whom there is no "other" whatsoever. The thirteen major Upanishads are the fountainhead of all expositions of Brahman.

Swami Nirmalananda illumines the Upanishads' practical value for spiritual seekers from the unique perspective of a lifetime of study and practice of both Eastern and Western spirituality.

The Bhagavad Gita–The Song of God

Often called the "Bible" of Hinduism, the Bhagavad Gita is found in households throughout India and has been translated into every major language of the world. Literally billions of copies have been handwritten or printed.

The clarity of this translation by Swami Nirmalananda makes for easy reading, while the rich content makes this the ideal "study" Gita. As the original Sanskrit language is so rich, often there are several accurate translations for the same word, which are noted in the text, giving the spiritual student the needed understanding of the fullness of the Gita.

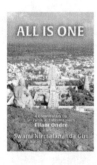

All Is One
A Commentary On Sri Vaiyai R. Subramanian's Ellam Ondre

"I you want moksha, read and practice the instructions in *Ellam Ondre*." Ramana Maharshi

Swami Nirmalananda's insightful commentary brings even further light to Ellam Ondre's refreshing perspective on what Unity signifies, and the path to its realization.

Written in the colorful and well-informed style typical of his other commentaries, it is a timely and important contribution to Advaitic literature that explains Unity as the fruit of yoga sadhana, rather than mere wishful thinking or some vague intellectual gymnastic, as is so commonly taught by the modern "Advaita gurus."

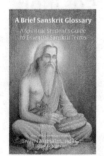

A Brief Sanskrit Glossary
A Spiritual Student's Guide to Essential Sanskrit Terms

This Sanskrit glossary contains full translations and explanations of hundreds of the most commonly used spiritual Sanskrit terms, and will help students of the Bhagavad Gita, the Upanishads, the Yoga Sutras of Patanjali, and other Indian scriptures and philosophical works to expand their vocabularies to include the Sanskrit terms contained in these, and gain a fuller understanding in their studies.

BOOKS ON ORIGINAL CHRISTIANITY

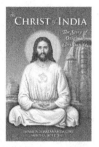

The Christ of India
The Story of Original Christianity

"Original Christianity" is the teaching of both Jesus and his Apostle Saint Thomas in India. Although it was new to the Mediterranean world, it was really the classical, traditional teachings of the rishis of India that even today comprise the Eternal Dharma, that goes far beyond religion into realization.

In *The Christ of India* Swami Nirmalananda presents what those ancient teachings are, as well as the growing evidence that Jesus spent much of his "Lost Years" in India and Tibet. This is also the story of how the original teachings of Jesus and Saint Thomas thrived in India for centuries before the coming of the European colonialists.

May a Christian Believe in Reincarnation?

Discover the real and surprising history of reincarnation and Christianity.

A growing number of people are open to the subject of past lives, and the belief in rebirth–reincarnation, metempsychosis, or transmigration–is commonplace. It often thought that belief in reincarnation and Christianity are incompatible. But is this really true? May a Christian believe in reincarnation? The answer may surprise you.

"Those needing evidence that a belief in reincarnation is in accordance with teachings of the Christ need look no further: Plainly laid out and explained in an intelligent manner from one who has spent his life on a Christ-like path of renunciation and prayer/meditation." —*Christopher T. Cook*

The Unknown Lives of Jesus and Mary
Compiled from Ancient Records and Mystical Revelations

"There are also many other things which Jesus did, the which, if they should be written every one, I suppose that even the world itself could not contain the books that should be written." (Gospel of Saint John, final verse)

You can discover much of those "many other things" in this unique compilation of ancient records and mystical revelations, which includes historical records of the lives of Jesus Christ and his Mother Mary that have been accepted and used by the Church since apostolic times. This treasury of little-known stories of Jesus' life will broaden the reader's understanding of what Christianity really was in its original form.

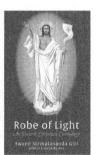

Robe of Light
An Esoteric Christian Cosmology

In *Robe of Light* Swami Nirmalananda explores the whys and wherefores of the mystery of creation. From the emanation of the worlds from the very Being of God, to the evolution of the souls to their ultimate destiny as perfected Sons of God, the ideal progression of creation is described. Since the rebellion of Lucifer and the fall of Adam and Eve from Paradise flawed the normal plan of evolution, a restoration was necessary. How this came about is the prime subject of this insightful study.

Moreover, what this means to aspirants for spiritual perfection is expounded, with a compelling knowledge of the scriptures and of the mystical traditions of East and West.

The Gospel of Thomas for Awakening
A Commentary on Jesus' Sayings as Recorded by the Apostle Thomas

When the Apostles dispersed to the various area of the world, Thomas travelled to India, where evidence shows Jesus spent his Lost Years, and which had been the source of the wisdom which he had brought to the "West."

The Christ that Saint Thomas quotes in this ancient text is quite different than the Christ presented by popular Christianity. Through his unique experience and study with both Christianity and Indian religion, Swami Nirmalananda clarifies the sometimes enigmatic sayings of Jesus in an informative and inspiring way.

The Odes of Solomon for Awakening
A Commentary on the Mystical Wisdom of the Earliest Christian Hymns and Poems

The Odes of Solomon is the earliest Christian hymn-book, and therefore one of the most important early Christian documents. Since they are mystical and esoteric, they teach and express the classical and universal mystical truths of Christianity, revealing a Christian perspective quite different than that of "Churchianity," and present the path of Christhood that all Christians are called to.

"Fresh and soothing, these 41 poems and hymns are beyond delightful! I deeply appreciate Abbot George Burke's useful and illuminating insight and find myself spiritually re-animated." John Lawhn

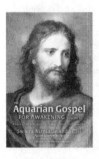

The Aquarian Gospel for Awakening (2 Volumes)
A Practical Commentary on Levi Dowling's Classic Life of Jesus Christ

Written in 1908 by the American mystic Levi Dowling, The Aquarian Gospel of Jesus the Christ answers many questions about Jesus' life that the Bible doesn't address. Dowling presents a universal message found at the heart of all valid religions, a broad vision of love and wisdom that will ring true with Christians who are attracted to Christ but put off by the narrow views of the tradition that has been given his name.

Swami Nirmalananda's commentary is a treasure-house of knowledge and insight that even further expands Dowling's vision of the true Christ and his message.

BOOKS ON BUDDHISM & TAOISM

The Dhammapada for Awakening
A Commentary on Buddha's Practical Wisdom

Swami Nirmalananda's commentary on this classic Buddhist scripture explores the Buddha's answers to the urgent questions, such as "How can I find find lasting peace, happiness and fulfillment that seems so elusive?" and "What can I do to avoid many of the miseries big and small that afflict all of us?" Drawing on his personal experience and on parallels in Hinduism and Christianity, the author sheds new light on the Buddha's eternal wisdom.

"Swami Nirmalananda's commentary is well crafted and stacked with anecdotes, humor, literary references and beautiful quotes from the Buddha. I found it to be entertaining as well as illuminating, and have come to consider it a guide to daily living." –Rev. Gerry Nangle

The Tao Teh King for Awakening
A Practical Commentary on Lao Tzu's Classic Exposition of Taoism

"The Tao does all things, yet our interior disposition determines our success or failure in coming to knowledge of the unknowable Tao."

Lao Tzu's classic writing, the Tao Teh King, has fascinated scholars and seekers for centuries. His presentation of the Tao which is the Eternal Reality, and the Way of the Sage that is the path to the realization of and dwelling in this Reality is illuminating, but its deeper meanings and practical applications remain obscure to many, especially in the West.

Swami Nirmalananda offers a commentary that makes the treasures of Lao Tzu's teachings accessible and applicable for the sincere seeker.

More Titles

The Four Gospels for Awakening

Light on the Path for Awakening

Wandering With a Cherubim: The Writings of Angelus Silesius

Psychic Defense for Yogis

Made in the USA
Coppell, TX
06 November 2023

23835910R00121